# MARKETING NEW REALITIES

## AN INTRODUCTION TO VIRTUAL REALITY & AUGMENTED REALITY MARKETING, BRANDING, & COMMUNICATIONS

CATHY HACKL

SAMANTHA G. WOLFE

THE MARKETING FUTURISTS

ISBN-13: 978-0-9965106-7-7

Editing by Megan LaFollett
Cover Design by Ashley Ruggirello

*To all the women in VR, AR and technology who are blazing the trail.*

# CONTENTS

There's always the question: How early should we get to the party?

The time is now. You are not too early. You are not too late.

> *When you see what furniture looks like in*
> *your house without buying a thing.*

> *When you can dive the Great Barrier Reef in*
> *the comfort of your own living room.*

> *When you can feel what it's like to be an addict*
> *without ever taking a drug or drink.*

> *When you are sitting in a fashion show in Paris*
> *on your lunch break in New York.*

> *When you're here and your team is there.*

Empathy. Adventure. Education. Experience. Immersion.

The virtual journey is now available to all.

How can you capture this opportunity as a brand?

It's possible.

The time is now.

From a perspective, never so readily available, by two authors—never so ready to take you there.

Say hello to *Marketing New Realities*. An Introduction to Virtual Reality and Augmented Reality, Marketing, Branding, & Communications by Cathy Hackl and Samantha G. Wolfe.

I'm happy to make this introduction to the next generation of this marketing revolution. After watching public relations mature into digital and morph into social media, it's exciting to see the revolutionary new view for you and your audience, a step out of 2D and into the possibilities of 3D and more.

Hackl and I met working together at the University of Florida in 2014 when she launched the first ever Periscope Summit. We've collaborated and experimented together with the rise of live video with a talk show called the Digital Dish. I've admired Hackl, an Emmy award-winning journalist, zero in on the AR/VR/MR marketing opportunity; and she has definitely brought it into fruition in this book. She's carried the torch from conference to conference, city to city, country to country, echoing the message the "time is coming, marketers need to be ready."

The time is now.

Hackl is joined by Wolfe, an award-winning marketing futurist specializing in emerging technologies. Together they peel back the complex layers of AR/VR/MR and simplify it into an actionable book with useful takeaways

Two global tech powerhouses, Hackl and Wolfe deliver a chapter-by-chapter playbook of how and when to use AR/VR technology for marketing. Doses of reality mixed with a twist of inspiration and backed with stats and facts. It's a cocktail of AR/VR success.

Read this book and you will be infused with a new reality for tomorrow's marketing. Most importantly, the who, what, where, when, and why to use AR/VR as a marketing strategy in a one-size fits all package.

They bring marketers the breadth and depth, cutting to the chase and filtering out the clutter.

That moment when you need to determine what AR/VR means for your brand. The inevitable questions: How does your brand promise extend to this medium? Is it worth it? What kind of experiences will enhance and improve your marketing campaigns? How can you surprise and delight your audience in new ways never before possible? How can you make this happen?

The time is now.

Hackl and Wolfe take you where you need to go.

The journey is just beginning, and you are here.

Let's immerse in the future of marketing today.


Namaste,

Author of *Social PR Secrets* and *Digital Detox Secrets* (coming 2018)

*THE FUTURE OF MARKETING IS HERE*

Virtual Reality (VR) and Augmented Reality (AR) are two of the biggest disruptors to ever hit the marketing and advertising industries. Couple that with the integration of Artificial Intelligence (AI), and the playing field has changed dramatically for everyone in the marketing, branding, and public relations sectors, from marketing managers to public relations directors to chief marketing officers.

The virtual future has arrived, and it's no longer science fiction. *Marketing New Realities* will help you navigate this new industry and give you the tools you need to create and manage successful marketing campaigns in the present, as well as prepare you for the years to come. We've divided the book into 5 main sections: Past, Present, Future, Far Future, and Practical Matters, in order to help you understand today's marketplace and contemplate the future of marketing and communications. Note that for simplicity's sake, we refer to you/the reader as a "Marketer" throughout the book. Let's dive in.

"What is real? How do you define 'real?' If you're talking about what you can feel, what you can smell, what you can taste and see, then 'real' is simply electrical signals interpreted by your brain."

Morpheus from *The Matrix*, 1999

When *The Matrix* movie came out 20 years ago, it was a mind-blowing experience questioning the nature of reality. But thinking about reality and trying to represent reality in new forms dates back hundreds of years.

THE 1830's MARKED THE FIRST SCIENTIFIC discoveries around understanding how the mind processes reality, as well as landmark attempts at recreating reality. Most notable was the discovery by Charles Wheatstone that the brain processes two slightly different images into one three-dimensional (3D) image. Three-dimensional (3D), or more accurately, "stereoscopic" content (Greek *stereos*, meaning "firm, solid," and *skopeo*, meaning "to look, to see"), has been documented as early as 1860, not long after the first daguerreotypes (photographs taken by an early photographic process, employing an iodine-sensitized silvered plate and mercury vapor).

In 1895, the Lumière brothers showed one of the first motion pictures in history, *Arrival of a Train at La Ciotat*, at a venue in Paris. Journalists at the time referred to it as "life caught in the act" and created the legend that viewers of the one-minute film ran out of the theater in fear. This is still considered one of the most important moments in the history of visual storytelling.[1]

Less than 43 years later, "la réalité virtuelle" was used in essays by a French multi-hypenate. A year later, an early precursor of the VR headset was patented. The View-Master was offered to consumers as "virtual tourism."

But it wasn't until 1987 that the term "Virtual Reality" was born. Although most people think that VR has only really been around for the past year or so, NASA has been using VR for more than 20 years to train astronauts and the U.S. military for training and flight simulations.

Fast forward to 2016, which is now commonly referred to by the gaming community as *Year One* of the birth of truly mainstream VR. (This is a comic-book reference to the famed rebirth of the *Batman* character, as reimagined by writer/director Frank Miller in *Batman: Year One*.)

As for the history of AR, the term "Augmented Reality" is believed to have been coined in 1992.[2] Boeing used AR to help workers assemble wires in their plane factory. In 1994, developers at the University of North Carolina at Chapel Hill created an augmented application to help doctors view a fetus within a pregnant patient. AR started to pick up some steam with very early adopters in the early 2010's, but never went mainstream. In 2016, with the release of Pokémon Go, the consumer potential of AR was showcased on a grand scale. As of September 2017, the app has been downloaded 752 million times, with $1.2 billion in revenue.[3]

If we use a corollary from mobile phone history, when it comes to VR and AR, we are somewhere in the brick cell phone days—when the technology was there, but it was bulky and we had no idea the impact it would have on our lives. With VR and AR, significant advancements have been made in the technologies, but we are far from understanding the true capabilities of either medium. It's an exciting and innovative time, with a ton of opportunities for VR/AR companies, brands, consumers, and for Marketers like you and us.

"Life moves pretty fast. If you don't stop and look around once in a while, you could miss it."

Ferris Bueller, 1986

Wise words from an 80's pop-culture truant. But the VR/AR industry is moving so fast that we need to take a second to pause and appreciate this exciting time of digital innovation and transformation, and to figure out how to best use the tools now available to us for branding and marketing. "Consumer demand, high-quality devices and market conditions have all aligned to make VR and AR the next major advancements in the tech world," states Eden Chen in a recent article in *Entrepreneur*.[4] This section will help you catch up on some of the details so you can start to take advantage of these new technologies.

BEFORE WE DIVE INTO THE TREMENDOUS POTENTIAL for marketing and advertising with VR and AR, now and in the future, we must first outline the definitions of the entire spectrum of technologies, and the current platforms they use. This includes Mixed Reality (MR), 360-video, Extended Reality (XR), and Holograms. It's crucial for you to understand what the differences are before planning your marketing campaigns.

It's helpful to consider all of these formats on a spectrum from least to most interactive: 360-video, Augmented Reality, Virtual Reality, Mixed Reality, to Holograms.

## *THE BASIC DEFINITIONS*

### 360-VIDEO: AN IMMERSIVE EXPERIENCE

360-Video is 2D video (or stereoscopic 3D) shot in 360-degrees that can be viewed on a headset or on a flat screen. It's what is most often associated with a Google Cardboard viewer. Think of it like a TV screen that you can look up/down/left/right/behind you. Sometimes people view it on a 2D screen and scroll up, down, left, and right to look around the 360-degrees. Sometimes it's viewed in a "magic window" format where you hold a mobile device, and it appears through the screen like you are in the 360-world. 360-video is most immersive in a headset where it feels like you are inside a TV globe.

As the viewer doesn't have agency to change the 360-video, it isn't technically VR. It's a director-led experience like TV. If you move your head inside of 360-video, it's not the perspective that changes, it's the part of the 360 sphere that is visible.

Another distinction is that with 360-video in a headset, you have 3DoF (3-degrees-of-freedom). So, if you kneel down, go to your left or right, or move forward or backwards, your point of view won't change. But, it will change if you tilt or turn your head.

In addition, there are developers pushing 180-degree view video instead of 360, where if you turn around you would only see black. It saves on production costs and rendering time, but it is less immersive. It was developed after observing that some people never look behind them when viewing content in 360. YouTube unveiled their support of VR180 formats at Vidcon 2017 and even released a camera with Google in June 2017, but the debate is still active. Most people have been choosing 360, as of now.

### VIRTUAL REALITY (VR): An Actively Immersive Experience

VR is a 360-degree virtual environment where you have the ability ("agency") to influence the world around you (e.g. move around the space, change the environment). The creator of VR must allow the user to be able to influence what happens.

VR is a fully immersive experience, which is usually attained by wearing a head mounted display (HMD). If you want to get even more technical, VR is supposed to let you have 6DoF (6-degrees-of-freedom). This is the technical term meaning that a user in a VR environment has the ability to move forward and backward ("surge"), up and down ("heave"), and left and right ("sway"), along with changes in where you can look and turn, which is on a normal axis ("yaw"), lateral axis ("pitch"), and longitudinal axis ("roll"). Basically, you are in a 3D world where you can move around wherever you like. In simple terms, VR creates new worlds to inhabit and experience.

## Augmented Reality (AR): *Enhanced Reality*

AR overlays graphics or video on top of what you see in the real world using computer vision and object recognition. The graphics can be seen on a phone or tablet or a headset where you can see *through* the headset (unlike VR where you only see what's presented on screen). AR can be fun, like Snapchat's viral Dancing Hot Dog. It can also bring utility and context to the world around you; for example, to help you determine what a piece of furniture looks like in your home. In simple terms, AR adds to your world.

## Mixed Reality (MR): *AR + Agency*

With MR, you can see the real world as well as graphics/video, and can interact with what you see. Mixed Reality is the term that companies like Microsoft and Magic Leap (one of the highest-funded startups in the history of startups) use to describe the next iteration beyond Augmented Reality. It's the next generation of AR & VR technologies, and what's often used in movies trying to showcase what the future will look like. For the purpose of this book, when we discuss VR and AR, MR is assumed to be part of that mix.

*EXTENDED REALITY (XR): VR, 360 Video, AR, and MR*
XR encompasses everything: 360-degree video, augmented, virtual, and mixed realities, and whatever other realities might be created in the future.

*HOLOGRAMS: 3D images made of light beams*
Humans have been obsessed with holographic content for a long time. Holographic content can be seen in movies from *Back to the Future*, to *Ghost in the Shell,* to *Blade Runner* and *Blade Runner 2049*. Alex Kipman, Technical Fellow at Microsoft, eloquently explains why holograms are the wave of the future during his TED talk *The Dawn of the Age of Holograms*, and why holographic content helps us go beyond the current 2D limitations and our ordinary range of perceptions, ushering in a new age of technology that amplifies the human experience and the way we all engage with the content around us. One of our favorite definitions of the term is from a 2016 article from *The Wall Street Journal.* "True holograms are 3D images produced by the interference of light beams that reflect off a real, physical object and can be seen with the naked eye. There are many different types of holograms."[5]

A major shift in content is happening as you read this. Marketers need to open their minds to move away from

2D/flat content to content that's 3D, 360/180 and some-times holographic. An indication of this shift is clear with Facebook's push to connect people across virtual and non-virtual worlds with the introduction of Facebook 3D posts. This effort was explained by Rachel Franklin, Head of Social VR at Facebook, during Oculus Connect 4: "With all the powerful content being created within VR, we're seeing the beginning of a new ecosystem. Users can use Oculus Medium to create new kinds of virtual content that is not confined to VR... Now objects created in VR can be shared in your newsfeed through the Facebook 3D post...any piece of Oculus Medium art can become a virtual object in Face-book Spaces. Soon you'll also be able to take a VR sculpture into AR and create an AR object using the Facebook camera and bring it into your real world."[6]

## THE BASIC TOOLS

Although the industry is evolving at a rapid pace, the following outlines the hardware that is available in 2017 to experience VR, AR, 360-Video, and MR.

### VR & 360-VIDEO: SMARTPHONES, TABLETS, & HEADSETS

There are a wide variety of Virtual Reality experiences available based upon the hardware used. The following outlines the different level of experiences:

#### ENTRY-LEVEL VR

The easiest point of entry is through 360-video. You can view this content on a computer or mobile screen, but it's not nearly as engaging as an immersive experience. The cheapest and easiest way, other than a flat 2D screen for scrolling or a magic window view, is to insert your phone into a cardboard viewer like Google Cardboard. A lot of Marketers use branded versions of these as giveaways with 360-video content.

## A BETTER VR EXPERIENCE

The next level of experience uses a headset that is custom-built for a smartphone. At this price point, you gain access to volume control, touch panels, and some focal adjustments. It also brings the flexibility of having one investment into a screen that can be used as a phone and a VR device with the right headset. Samsung and Google dominate the market in 2017 with the Samsung Gear VR and the Google Daydream View for the Google Pixel 1 and 2 Phone. The Daydream View is also compatible with Huawei's Mate 9 Pro. Both Samsung and Google's offerings are "walled gardens" though; they have content that's only available on that particular headset. Again, as an example of how they might be used in marketing, these types of headsets tend to be used at pop-up event activations.

Recently there has been a lot of talk of an internet-based VR/360-video experience for mobile headsets, rather than downloaded applications. This distribution method, called WebVR, allows for universal access across mobile headsets. As of the writing of this book, the Firefox browser has the first mover advantage, but Google Chrome recently announced support of WebVR. This delivery method is just in its infancy and isn't as reliable as downloaded apps, but as there is so much interest, we expect it to grow quickly.

## THE BEST VR EXPERIENCE

A true VR experience requires a dedicated set of hardware. VR at this level has movement tracking and the ability to "touch" objects (known as haptic capability). Companies such as HTC, Oculus, Dell, HP, Asus, Lenovo, and Sony have focused on this platform. In 2017, all of these are tethered (i.e. you have a big cord hanging off of your headset that's attached to a console), and you need a high-powered computer with a high-performing graphics card that can handle the applications, or a game console in the case of Sony's Playstation VR. But our hope is that by 2018, this will no longer be necessary for all VR headsets. This type of headset, besides home and arcade use, is often integrated into trade events or large activations (e.g. SXSW), where the full VR experience is necessary to make a deep impact with attendees.

## VR ACCESSORIES

True VR can also incorporate a wide variety of add-ons to further enhance the VR experience and make it feel more real. All of these tools vary dramatically in price, quality, and availability. While by no means complete, here is a list of some of them for easy reference, in case you want to add a little extra to your own VR experience or event:

- Audio strap: Allows for built-in headphones to be attached to headgear.
- Force Feedback Vest: Feel thuds and vibrations on your chest.
- Handheld controllers (varies by system)
- Rudder: A foot-based round controller.

- VR Bike: An exercise bike with controllers attached to the VR experience.
- VR Chair: Rotating chair with feedback and foot pedals.
- VR Cover: For sanitary reasons.
- VR Treadmill: Omnidirectional treadmills that move in 360 degrees. Austin-based Virtuix is one of the top VR treadmills on the market.
- VIVE Trackers: A puck that helps map movements in VR.

In Development and/or Available Soon:

- Foot pads
- Full-body haptic suits
- Glove controllers (like Atlanta-based, VR Gluv)
- Reactive grip controllers
- VR Scent (smell-o-vision): This technology was demoed at Tribeca Film Festival in the VR experience *Treehugger: Wawona*, where users could feel and smell a redwood tree in VR.

Each can add a distinctive twist to your marketing creative, and they can be used in combination.

*AR HARDWARE: Smartphone or Tablet*

Augmented Reality is available through a smartphone or tablet. People within the industry anticipate that AR will start to take off in late 2017. Why? The next generation of Apple phones and tablets have ARKit built into them, which will allow more AR opportunities for developers and therefore better AR apps for consumers. Google's ARCore is also hoping to make a major impact in the adoption of AR apps by Android users. You already think you're addicted to your phone? Just wait.

Google Glass (which many consider AR glasses) was an early mover in the consumer AR space when it launched 2014. It was taken off the market, and then relaunched as a business solution. The new product works with existing eyewear for industries and is being sold as a solution for medical and agricultural and manufacturing industries, etc.

## MIXED REALITY: *Headsets*

Mixed Reality headsets are used by developers and companies willing to spend for event activations. Microsoft introduced the Microsoft Hololens in 2016, while Meta, an AR startup from Silicon Valley, has started shipping its Meta 2 developer's kit. Both MR headsets bring a futuristic view of how MR will progress from handsets (our phones) to headsets. (If you listen to Meta's CEO, Meron Gribetz's TED Talk you can better understand why, in the future, smart eyewear will help us reconnect as humans.)

Price drops in this space should make MR more mainstream in the coming months or years. Other brands like Osterhouse Design Group (ODG), Atheer, Epson (Moverio), and Mira Realities are all innovating in the MR glasses or headsets sector. Additionally, Snap (parent company of Snapchat) is expected to have MR incorporated into the next iteration of their Snap Spectacles. Many in the industry are still waiting to see what Magic Leap will come to market with in this arena. A lot of companies are working with MR headsets now, in anticipation of quick consumer adoption.

ften underestimate the power of sound when it comes to visual mediums. Beyond just being able to hear people clearly, sound effects, ambience, and a musical score can do much to heighten the experience of cinema, games, and immersion. But most importantly to VR directors, it draws the audience's attention. Without the ability to pull focus in VR, binaural (2 ear) 3D audio allows the director to point the audience to the next piece of important content. Google calls it "a key element for an immersive virtual reality experience," and they launched Omnitone, which is an open source spatial audio project in support of the need for high quality audio.[7]

Richard Marks, senior director of research and development at Sony Computer Entertainment America, said, "While purely visual VR experiences can be made, adding 3D audio greatly magnifies the impact and depth of a VR experience."[8] Spatial audio is more advanced than surround sound, as it recreates the direction of the sound based on the perception of sound from each ear.

Proper spatial audio in immersive content can make or break the experience. If the audio can change positioning when you move your head, the feeling of immersion increases. The highest end audio experiences even include inter-aural time difference (the time difference between each of your ears when hearing a sound), environmental reflections (the sound reflections from surfaces such as walls and floors), and filtering of sounds based on your body (ex. the shape of your ear). Compare the same content played back to stereo or surround audio vs. spatial audio, and it becomes abundantly clear that stereo isn't how we hear the world in real life.

## DISTRIBUTION

Often one of the first things that comes up in any discussion about VR and AR is how many people actually use it. The answer varies based on the type of experience you develop. 360-video has a much wider distribution than VR. AR via Snapchat Lenses is huge, AR technology (ARKit, ARCore) will be widely integrated into smartphones, and a significant number of AR apps are going to be launched within the next few months to a year.

As a quick reference, here are the product sales numbers available to the public as of late summer 2017:

- 10 Million: Google Cardboards shipped,[9] with significantly more millions given away (estimated 88.4 Million total players)[10] and 160 million downloads of Cardboard apps[11]

- 8 Million: Gear VR units sold[12]

- 1.8 Million: PlayStation VR units sold[13]

- 667 Thousand: HTC Vive headsets sold[14]

- 383 Thousand: Oculus Rifts sold[15]

As for how to distribute the content itself besides embedding it into your own website, you can post your videos to YouTube 360 (which is coming to over-the-top TV platforms), Facebook 360, and Vimeo 360. You can also submit to Littlstar (which is expanding into AR as well), Jaunt, Hulu, Within, storefronts within each hardware solu-

Samsung), and film festivals to see if they will ur video. There is also the option of creating an app and placing it in mobile app stores.

You may be saying, "Thanks for that, but, Cathy and Sam, how many people will use my VR or AR creative, if I make it?" When it comes to VR, you need to think beyond the reach of VR headsets in homes; it can be used at B2B or B2C events, as a way to get press, and you can create 360-video and 2D versions of your content to get wider distribution. AR is more of a mass play, but you still need to drive people to use it. Some companies think they just need to create one VR or AR experience and then drop their mic. VR and AR need to be integrated into a larger cross-platform campaign to be effective.

## FINANCIAL OPPORTUNITY

The opportunity for VR and AR is huge. As a reference, here are some financial forecasts for the industry as a whole:

- *Fast Company* estimates that VR and AR will generate $150 billion in revenue by 2020.[16]

- *Digi-Capital* predicts that mobile augmented reality might become the primary driver of a $108 billion VR/AR market by 2021. Out of which $83 billion would be claimed by AR.[17]

- Superdata Research predicts the hardware and software market for VR to reach $28.3 billion in 2020.[18]

- IDC forecasts that worldwide revenues for Augmented and Virtual Reality will reach $162 billion in 2020.[19]

- Goldman Sachs research expects virtual and augmented reality to become an $80 billion market by 2025, roughly the size of the desktop PC market today.[20]

All of these numbers will change rapidly, as will consumer attitudes, making the discussion of total audience lower on the agenda. It will be more of a question of what VR/AR experiences your brand needs, not *if* you will be doing one.

## 3 / SOCIAL & ADVERTISING CONNECTIONS

VR AND AR HAVE BEEN BIRTHED OUT OF SOCIAL MEDIA powerhouses and Fortune 500 advertisers. Facebook, YouTube, Instagram, Twitter, and Snapchat are some of the companies that are funding a large number of VR and AR advancements, beyond the hardware manufacturers.

There are now 2 billion users on Facebook, a staggering 25% of the entire population of the planet Earth. 95% of all the revenue it generated in 2016 was from ads: about $27 Billion USD.[21] If we place that number into perspective, Facebook makes more revenue than the GDP of the bottom 100 of the approximately 260 recognized countries in the world.

Facebook bought out Oculus in order to take over control of its development, and is supporting a diverse group of content creators who are developing content for the Oculus Store. For example, Facebook is already merging social networking with virtual reality (social VR) by enabling users to use emojis to "like" 360-degree VR videos while wearing their headsets.

Of course, Facebook is not the only company with skin in the game. We need look no further than the first of the artificially intelligent ad-serving companies, Google. For the year of 2016, Google earned nearly $80 billion USD in revenue from ads.[22] It also wanted its slice of the VR/AR pie. Google partnered with the mobile company HTC to create a VR-lite version with a smartphone with an adapter: the Daydream. (Eventually making a $1.1 billion dollar offer for the company in September of 2017).[23] Google's parent company, Alphabet, also owns YouTube. YouTube created a dedicated VR app for Daydream. They already support 360-degree/VR video on desktop, mobile devices, and Google Cardboard.

Although they haven't made billion-dollar investments, Snapchat has been at the forefront of AR with their Lenses and Frames. They consistently offer more filters and had a viral success with their dancing hot dog, which is now known as the "first Augmented Reality superstar."[24] Last year, Snapchat's parent company Snap, Inc., launched Spectacle glasses (positioning them as a toy, unlike Google Glass). Many expect the next version of Spectacles to include AR. Snapchat also worked in conjunction with Apple for the exceptional facial tracking lenses that can only be accessed via the iPhone X.

Snapchat is one of the top social media networks to watch as immersive technologies, especially AR, progress. Snap has partnered with New York-based Entrypoint, a 360-video web player focused on making 360 content accessible, shareable, and interactive. Through the partnership, the player enables content creators to use interactive features like picture-in-picture (overlaying a 2D video on a 360 one), and to create short shareable GIFs that link directly back to that moment in the video through

Snapchat. In addition, Snapchat launched 360-advertising last year.

As for the rest of the social media landscape:

- *Instagram*: The Facebook-owned company only has some AR frames and masks, but as tech progresses we will probably see 360 videos and photos come to life.

- *Twitter*: The company has been making several hires for their VR/AR push, but they haven't announced their VR/AR strategy. They have integrated 360-degree video and 360-degree video live streaming via Twitter's Periscope app.

Besides being really fascinating and cool technologies (although we are biased on that front), what has prompted these companies to invest millions into VR, 360-video, and AR technologies?

Advertising. The revenue potential for VR and AR is huge. It opens a way to market to users in ways heretofore never imagined. These companies don't want to be left behind, so they're placing their various stakes in this new frontier of the Wild West Gold Rush.

Media companies like The Gannett Company's USA Today Network are experimenting with and implementing VR advertising. According to a *Marketing Land* article, the network has partnered with Nielsen to measure the impact of VR on brand metrics.[25] In the same article, Kelly Andresen, SVP and head of GET Creative at USA Today Network said: "It's an amazing medium for advertising, likely because it's so immersive people remember the content and VR has a 2x brand recall compared to TV."

There are some interesting tidbits about Facebook's play in the sector, known currently as Oculus Rift, that need to be considered. For example: anything you make using Oculus' services, can be used by Facebook.[26] When you enter the metaverse (the virtual worlds of cyberspace), everything you listen to, visit, where you look in these worlds and for how long, even what you speak or chat, will be recorded and stored and can be used for advertisers on and off their services. Just checkout the Terms of Service for Oculus Rift.

Although it feels like "Big Brother" is watching, this allows for tremendous targeting opportunities for advertisers. Digital advertising campaigns can already track you and then reach you at your most primed purchasing moment. Advertising in a VR/AR world brings a literal extra dimension to these targeting efforts.

## REAL ADVERTISING

There is a reason why AR and VR use the term "reality." These 3D worlds and 3D objects appear and seem real to the naked eye. In true VR, the system tracks your body, hands, and head movements in 3D space, so your mind is tricked into a sense of greater immersion understood as "presence." One's perception of an event becomes more real, even if the video/graphic representation being shown is not necessarily photorealistic.

As an advertiser or marketer, the more closely a consumer can identify with your brand or product(s), the more likely they are to remain loyal customers. Although behavioral patterns can be determined based on Snaps,

Facebook posts, search engine requests, and TV viewing habits, it's only with in-person research studies that marketers can get a complete picture. VR will allow for a full picture of consumer behavior. And AR will show how consumers interact with and use products.

As marketers, we are concerned with recall of our brands. Will someone remember what our service or product is named? Will the brand be in the consideration set for purchase? As of October 2017, there haven't been many studies about VR/AR and brand recollection, but here are some references for extrapolation:

- Nielsen and Airpush conducted a VR ad effectiveness study and found that ads in VR were more effective by 1.5 to 18x depending on the content and metric, brand recall was 8x more effective, and 2x more likely to share.[27]

- In Snapchat, sponsored lenses increased ad awareness by 19.7 points and brand awareness by 6.4 points.[28]

- YuMe researched the emotional engagement of 360-video in a headset vs. 360-video on a flat screen vs. 2D video. In a headset was 27% more emotionally engaging than 2D, and flat 360-video was 17% higher.[29]

- YuMe also found viewers engaged 34% longer in a headset and 16% longer with flat 360-video than the same content in 2D.[30]

So, what does all of this mean to advertising in the metaverse? The artist Keiichi Matsuda made a six-minute short depicting a dystopian view a mixed-reality future. The video, aptly entitled *Hyper-Reality*, is about how our AR-enhanced worlds are infiltrated with ads 24/7/365 and how that could be a very overwhelming and frustrating experience.

It's our job as Marketers, advertisers, and PR professionals to develop guardrails to make sure this doesn't happen, especially as there aren't yet any established standards or codes of behavior. (See John Bucher's book, *Storytelling for Virtual Reality: Methods and Principles for Crafting Immersive Experiences*). In fact, the IAB (the Interactive Advertising Bureau) released their first set of guidelines this year for VR and AR. The VR/AR Association (VRARA) and several of its committees are actively working on also creating best practices for this new discipline.

There are a lot of considerations when it comes to advertising in the metaverse:

### VOLUME

What is the right amount of advertising that should be allowed? Researchers are just now digging into the effectiveness of certain formats. Consumers are more aware of advertising if they are in an experience or interacting with an AR graphic. If consumers are interacting with brands and within branded worlds, consider how you might react in the "real world" if you had the powers that VR and AR bring.

In order to not be overwhelmed by advertising in a VR/AR world, some individuals may pay for the privilege of privacy. Others will have to agree to the marketing as a means to subsidize the cost of the device and its connectivity, or, ideally, as they don't find relevant advertising to be obtrusive (fingers crossed here).

## 360-TV ON STEROIDS

We've seen how social media has increased bullying. VR and AR are still relatively new media, although the technology has been around for a while. Until there are industry rules or common laws, we should strive to make Virtual and Augmented Reality a safe place that reflects a more utopian vs. dystopian vision. Here is what we propose as considerations for Marketers:

- *Length of viewing*: The current recommended length is 5 to 20 minutes.

- *Low volume*: Try and keep advertising to a minimum.

- *Pro-social*: When possible, encourage pro-social, not anti-social behavior.

- *Relevant*: Don't have advertising that's distracting; instead have it enhance the experience.

- *Safeguards*: Discourage certain behavior and use; add in warnings about upsetting or violent imagery; include age advisories.

Why is this important? Because of the powerful emotions that immersive experiences elicit, compared to a

2D universe. Yes, that holiday TV commercial may mal
you tear up, but you won't feel like you were in the room
with the characters. You won't remember it like your own
memories. In VR and AR, there will be shoot 'em up experiences and bone-chilling horror executions, but we should
create and promote these powerful experiences knowing
our moral obligations to each other and our society. We
don't advocate censoring, but we recommend Marketers
treat VR/AR as an extremely impactful media, like TV
or film on steroids.

## ADAPTING EXISTING CREATIVE

On a lighter note, although you might think it will be easier
and cheaper to "cut and paste" the creative you already have
into VR and AR, the result will be awkward and may reflect
poorly on your brand. 2D ads and graphics could lessen the
immersion felt by users.

Think about how to use the medium in new and
different ways. How can your creative have volume? How
can you interact with it? How could you get a user to move
around and look in different directions other than just in
front of them?

## 4 / THE EMPATHY MACHINE

THERE IS A FAMOUS PROVERB: "DON'T JUDGE A [person], until you walk a mile in [his/her] shoes." This speaks to the importance of empathy. Empathy involves the identification and understanding of the other's situation, feelings, or motives, because we have experienced the same thing. But is it ever really possible to walk in someone else's shoes?

VR technology enables experiential presence, and therefore, literally to feel like you are in someone else's shoes. In VR, it's all about the experience. Because of this, VR is often referred to as an "empathy machine." (To clarify, *well-produced*, high-quality VR can be a way to elicit empathy with open-minded viewers). Some within the VR industry don't like the term "empathy machine," as not *all* VR will make you feel something; but really good VR makes you feel significantly more than a 2D viewing experience.

As Marketers, why is empathy important? It has been found that the "most effective way to maximize customer value is to move beyond mere customer satisfaction and connect with customers at an emotional level—tapping into their fundamental motivations and fulfilling their deep, often unspoken emotional needs."[31] Customers move along an "emotional connection pathway" from being unconnected to satisfaction to differentiation to connection. We hypothesize that the empathy machine speeds consumers down this connection pathway to reach consumers emotionally.

Non-profits and cause marketers have begun to capitalize on this opportunity. Journalistic organizations also have prioritized 360-Video and VR to amplify the reach of their stories and to better connect with their readers/viewers.

One of the companies focused on VR journalism is called RYOT. Their tagline is: "Catalyzing the future of media by inviting our audience to be more than a witness." Learning about the plight of people from Guatemala becomes far more engaging when you feel as if you're standing shoulder-to-shoulder with them right there, in the moment. RYOT has created videos for *The New York Times*, NPR, the Associated Press, *Huffington Post*, and the Sierra Club.

Another company focused on human-centric storytelling is Within. It creates, collaborates, and distributes premium 360-video in a variety of genres. They've used the medium to tell stories about understanding those stuck in the cycle of mass incarceration and its high recidivism rates, or bearing witness to the trials of a day in the life of a Syrian refugee. The stories become so much more than just a headline, a lower third, or a talking head with a few unrelated contextual video clips.

Might the very technology that is dominated by men be used to help that very demographic understand what it's like to be a woman, a member of a minority group, or to better understand their LGBTQ counterparts? The interactive performance art piece, *The Machine To Be Another* from Barcelona-based BeAnotherLab, is about swapping gender and/or ethnicity with another person who is at the same time engaged in mirroring your activities in VR (although there is a similar traveling experience that uses CGI and prosthetic mannequins).

Embodying the physical perspective of a character, being present in the situation, and being able to witness it from both sides, can be an incredibly eye-opening experience. Because you're likely to remember VR as if you were there in real life, it might stir within you enough compassion to act. It's possible that VR may have the ability to flip the mirror of humanity unto itself.

## ANIMATED OPPORTUNITY

On the lighter side, animation in VR has some companies creating wonderful, ground-breaking creative pieces. Baobob Studios has the Emmy Award winning *Invasion!*, and their newest, the interactive *Asteroids!*. In each, you feel far more emotionally connected with the cute characters than with any 2D visual (with the possible exception of a couple Pixar films). Penrose Studios *Arden's Wake* shows not only a complete grasp of what's possible in VR, but it makes you feel like you've dropped into an alternative animated universe with characters that you love almost immediately. And Google Spotlight Stories' Oscar-nominated *Pearl* demonstrates how to tell a 360 story beautifully.

Although companies like Baobob and Penrose aren't plastering logos across their amazing creative, Marketers experiencing the emotional resonance and technology of these short films can see the amazing possibilities of VR. Brands and agencies can translate (or even fund, sponsor, or tastefully integrate) into groundbreaking original creative to utilize this empathy machine.

## EMPATHY & AR

While empathy and AR are still a bit of a nascent field, there are already several companies like Empathetic Computing Labs and Empathetic Media exploring how AR can be used to generate compassion and empathy. Empathetic Media, led by Dan Archer, in collaboration with the ATTeam from the Red Cross Pancevo (part of the Red Cross Serbia), created #STOPtrafficking2016 to raise awareness about the issue of modern human trafficking. The AR experience was released on July 30, 2016, as part of the World Day Against Trafficking in Persons, and explores the issue through the stories of three people directly affected by it. It brilliantly uses traffic stop signs as triggers, and users can go up to a real-world stop sign or a graphic of one to view the story.

"These aren't the droids you're looking for."

Obi-Wan Kenobi, *Star Wars*

Let's face it. Obi-Wan would have been a marketing genius. But without the ability to read and manipulate the minds of consumers, marketers have to use research, see what consumers and our competitors are doing, and then make a choice. Luckily, the future of marketing incorporates more flexibility than before, and, even better, you have the following chapters to help you future-proof as much as possible when it comes to VR/AR.

WHY DID SNAPCHAT'S DANCING HOT DOG GO VIRAL? Why did so many people run around looking for Pokémon? Because it's enjoyable (and a bit powerful) to alter your environment and see something that only people "in the know" can see. You become a bit of a Superman or Superwoman. But, even at the launch of the new iPhone and AR apps in 2017, the technology has begun to mature beyond fun and games.

Augmented Reality can offer utility and helps contextualize consumers' realities significantly more than other media. This means that marketing and sales will need to adapt, especially when it comes to social media and content marketing. AR can provide a reason for consumers to check out your brands and stores. It will change the way you can tell stories to engage with your customers.

This is only the tip of the iceberg. AR marketing provides a wide range of experiences and possibilities. With AR more accessible than ever, brands now can understand their customers in greater depth: from how they find new products to how they decide which one to buy. Marketers can create new experiences that increase engagement and loyalty. And all of this will start with your customers' mobile phones, and eventually move to AR headsets/glasses.

## SHOPPING SHIFTS INTO VR/AR

Consumers are a fickle bunch. One day they're hot for one product, and then the following week or month later, they've forgotten all about it. In the tech industry more than others, consumers will go out of their way for products that are a "must have," going so far as trampling each other at special sales during the holidays.

Google, Apple, Amazon, and other e-commerce sites have changed consumer behavior on a truly massive scale over the past twenty years. We have gone from hesitantly entering our debit or credit cards, to linking our ACH (Automatic Clearing House) directly to these behemoths, simply because of the frictionless shopping experience they provide.

The ability to buy goods online for less than at a mom and pop store, to purchase them in bulk for the savings that provides, or to wirelessly download the latest catchy tune in seconds, is now our way of life.

Anything that isn't that simple to transact is at a huge friction cost. A Google-conducted study showed that most people won't wait more than an average of three seconds for a web page to load on any device before moving on to something else.[32]

Malls, once the meeting place of moody teenagers seeking to escape school or their home for just a few hours, have been closing at a devastating pace. Many are quick to throw blame and state, "the Millennials did it," but it's simply not the case. Everyone's shopping habits have shifted to online over the past two decades, which began before the first Millennials of that generation were born. That's right, Baby Boomers and Gen X-ers, it's time for a look in the virtual mirror.

There has been no lack of resistance to that shift in shopping behavior. Macy's spent millions in a transparent move to attract Millennials that didn't just backfire, it went wholly unnoticed by the very demographic it eagerly sought to court. Malls used to be a place to be entertained. Now, with the entirety of the planet's content in the palm of one's hand, malls have to integrate the social and virtual communities into their physical spaces to garner any remaining attention at all.

It's no longer a secret that Amazon and AliBaba are already preparing, testing, and designing the WebVR/3D versions of their future websites. If you think going to your local supermarket is still a chore, look at how this video depicts a modern mom doing her shopping from home using VR: bit.ly/shelfzone.

In Alibaba's "Buy+," they are creating what appears to be an AR experience, but is really a photorealistic, fictional VR mall, depicted through stylized interaction via AR smart-glasses, as seen in this demo: bit.ly/vidVRshop.

It may seem a bit counter-intuitive to recreate a mall in VR, and then use it as the portal for people to do their VR shopping. However, the user experience (UX) takes into consideration current consumer behavior. It would not make sense to completely abstract the VR experience with only floating 3D simulations of real objects for sale.

Secondly, even though people now habitually spend more time at their homes, they remain social—introverts more so in VR.[33] These simulated, familiar spaces are areas where people not only shop, but they can congregate and mingle. If anything, the more entertaining and/or gamified the VR experience, as shown in the Alibaba demo, it's logical that the stickier the VR website shopping tends to be, and the more likely purchases are to be made. Additionally, even though people may be sharing a space contemporaneously, advertisements and other kinds of preferences will appear catered only to their version of the VR mall's shared locations. This can be subtly used to constantly and positively reinforce a consumer's association to a brand over time.

Does it come as any surprise that forward-thinking companies such as IKEA, pondering the possibility of how the future of retail may make their "big box" locations irrelevant, have entered *both* the VR and AR spaces, with apps of their own? IKEA VR is already here: bit.ly/ikeaVR. Believe it or not, the IKEA AR experience goes back as far as 2013. It began with their catalog acting as a "trigger marker" for your mobile device, in order to pick and decorate your home with a preview!

Interestingly, it's the faux AR experience in VR from Alibaba, and the AR example from IKEA, that demonstrate how brick and mortar may have a future. Yet, that may be entirely too dependent on the technology evolving fast enough, while dropping in price, in time to become more mainstream.

In 2013, companies like Cisco and Microsoft issued AR "mirrors" for auto-fitting and suggesting clothing. Collected data could be stored indefinitely and even shared socially for recommendations from friends, but it never really seemed to catch on. Even as the Internet of Things (IoT) hit a fever pitch in 2015, interactive and animated video displays of larger than life size did little more than make people stop for a moment before moving on with their day.

A gamified shopping mall environment with social experiences might be key to attracting and retaining foot traffic with sales, but the learning curve for both consumers and retailers might be too steep, and too little, too late. Given the earlier attempts with connected stores, AR mirrors, and interactive video storefronts, the closing of a huge number of modern retail spaces worldwide might prove inevitable; but the possibility of integrated AR does offer a glimmer of hope.

For example, all these interactions, sales, social information, etc. in VR and AR can be stored and cross-referenced to aid in future sales, incentives, or cross-promotions at another store that may be owned by a larger corporate parent or partner. In the virtual world, all the consumer's preferences for browsing, colors, materials, fabrics, designers, style, etc., can be tailored for every individual, making their experiences with a brand exceptional at every opportunity, even as their tastes change over time.

On the AR front, Atlanta-based You Are Here worked with client Porsche to create an AR app for iOS that customers or enthusiasts can use to create their own customized Porsche model and even see how the vehicle would look on their driveway, even before they set foot inside a dealership.

Also, NY-based YouVisit partnered with Masterpass and Swarovski to create one of the first V-Commerce experiences that offered a checkout option in VR. In it, consumers can tour Swarovski's high-end Atelier Collection via VR and can purchase items directly without the need to remove their headsets.

It quickly becomes hard to debate that most brands

would not eventually benefit from VR and AR. Both can personalize each customer experience with pricing, recommendations, virtual shopping carts, and Easter egg discounts hidden within the store. The sheer cost of creating, maintaining, and adapting retail spaces to compete with the virtual versions, will likely prove unsustainable if married to traditional operational models. The present of shopping and brands is AR; the future is VR.

## AR ADVERTISING

Augmented Reality changes the way we view the world, and it enhances our surroundings. But the question for marketers and brands is, how are we going to reach consumers with AR?

Brands saw an increase in ROIs, followers, purchases, and other means skyrocket with social media. When first launched, Facebook wasn't conceived initially as a platform to engage with potential customers. Last year, in a new world record, people consumed more media than ever before: over 10 hours and 39 minutes per day.[34] "Marketers will need to seriously examine the immersive space going forward to gauge whether content created in these mediums fits their needs at all," according to Rob Holzer, CEO of Matter Unlimited, a creative agency in New York.[35] AR will push this usage even further.

AR is set to be a new trillion-dollar industry and growing, according to AdAge.[36] It will enrich how we receive information such as dates, names, places, and ideas around us. Each AR experience will be tailored, and brands are catching on to marketing benefits. Brands such as Snapchat and Apple have already started to use AR to catch the attention of their customers. Users are able to scan codes via

AR to see real-life data or animations appear on their screens.

What AR experience would be right for your product, idea, or company name? It needs to be on-brand and increase awareness and/or retention. According to Adweek, in order for a brand's work to stand out, it has to have a reason and purpose to be there.[37] It has to be part of the story and part of the reason why consumers are going to engage with it. That is the challenge facing us as marketers in the coming years. A study by Tractica estimates that ad revenue in AR is projected to grow from $68 million last year to $13 billion in 2022.[38]

As AR primarily uses smartphones, Chuck Martin, editor at *MediaPost*, highlights that one of the enablers of the large growth is the sheer number in use.[39] By the end of this year, there are expected to be more than 3 billion smartphone users. With more Augmented Reality apps launching, AR will be available to the masses, which may not even notice they are using AR as it will become so commonplace.

In order to successfully reach their target audience, brands must understand *and* anticipate users' interaction with technology more than ever before. Consumer research and tracking will be essential in development of campaigns. Does your target audience for your beauty company enjoy full-body AR, where they look like they are applying makeup at their favorite beauty store, or do they prefer a simpler experience? AR is meant to enhance what your customers already know about your brand.

Currently, AR technology is primarily available on smartphones and other mobile devices. That will soon change. Many tech companies agree that AR will transition into headsets and smart glasses. This hardware will increase the usability of AR, and your augmented environment will no longer be limited to just what is on your phone screen. You will be able to survey everything around you with AR as a guide. Some have said that Google Glass was ahead of its time, but the market is ready now to receive AR into their world. Current AR headset options are expensive, tethered, or provide a limited field of view, but as more consumers start using AR on their phones they will want to move away from looking down at a screen.

Already, brands are using technology to capture the attention of the shopper. The vice president of Blippar, Lisa Hu, said in an interview that AR campaigns have an average dwell time of 75 seconds—this is 2.5 times the average of radio or TV ads.[40] AdAge interprets this length of usage as AR enhancing the lives of customers while simplifying their overall retail experience.[41] AR will also create an easier way of gathering analytics and observing shopping behaviors. "For example, both Wal-Mart and Target are in the process of testing augmented reality apps that would provide the user with in-store navigation, allowing for faster shopping time and less frustration. This type of improved customer experience can lead to increased customer loyalty, higher retention numbers and more repeat sales" (Con+ent).[42]

Marketing with AR goes hand in hand with the user shopping experience. If the user is looking for a new pair of shoes, imagine them lifting their phone up to any shoes they already have and a list of the consumer's favorite pairs appears on the screen, and virtually trying them on. It's all about taking the consumer's experience that they are having already and transforming it to the brand's world. Look at Snapchat and how different companies, brands, musicians, event coordinators, actors, etc. use their own filters and information to change what we already see. If a user can be browsing online looking for a new house to purchase, a real estate AR app can advise them there is a house nearby that fits their criteria for sale, and offer an opportunity to virtually see the home in a 3D environment (and themselves within it). This same type of experience applies to a tourist who visits another country. The user can simply download an AR travel app, put in their preferences, and find the nearest coffee shop with real-time directions and information about the relevant stores they pass layered upon their screen.

Logically, as the industry grows, businesses will begin to pay AR platforms for ad space and featured positions on applications and software. Companies targeting the users like the ones mentioned above will want to guarantee that people see their company's ad, increasing the chance to turn those AR users into customers. Serial entrepreneur Kristopher Jones points out that product placement remains an important factor to consider when it comes to AR advertising. He says that, "not unlike high traffic areas such as Times Square or Santa Monica Boulevard where brands spend tens of thousands of dollars on advertising, augmented reality presents a new way for brands to get in front of potentially engaged users. Big brands need to become part of the reality experienced in new virtual or augmented worlds or they will be replaced by imaginary or new, innovative marketers."[43]

But brand managers shouldn't get distracted by the technology. Matt Szymczyk, CEO of Zugara, an AR company, says that, "AR should be used to enhance content —not replace it. The main challenge is understanding that AR is not a digital strategy but rather a digital tactic that can enhance a campaign across multiple platforms."[44] Share of voice will be key, as brands will need to find a way to stand out, but not overwhelm, users.

In a guest post for Cisco, Zappar's VP of Business Development, Keith Curtin, stated that "products and objects are going to become next-generation websites filled with 3D content that users can touch, hold, speak to, and learn from. This entirely new medium will give brands and advertisers the ability to engage with—and learn about—their consumers in ways that never existed before. It will close the gap between the physical and digital, allowing brands to create platforms and communities that far exceed limitations posed through today's existing media channels. This will also profoundly impact product sales, brand loyalties, and consumer engagement at unimaginable rates."[45]

Virtual Reality has certainly captured the attention of Hollywood and advertisers. However, producing a major motion picture, mass market TV show, or an advertising content campaign entirely in the format has not yet been achieved. However, many have been getting their feet wet, mostly by using 360 and VR as a marketing tool. Several in the industry have also started using the term "storyliving" to better explain how one experiences VR.

## VR PRODUCTION & DISTRIBUTION

Right now, producing content in VR is significantly more complex and more expensive than 2D, but greater consumer demand and technological advancements will reduce the differential. When comparing 2D video to VR, there are more considerations and more expensive gear, like a high-end head-mounted-display (HMD) that has trackers for room-scale VR productions. The amount of data being used to create and deliver VR is much larger, and phones don't yet have the proper resolution or pixel density to support true VR. Luckily, everyone in the VR industry is aware of the issue, and companies are addressing it directly.

So if you have tried VR, but you found it to be a little fuzzy or blurry, be assured that will change. When it does, it will make a significant impact on the presence you feel within the VR experience. It is important for studios to communicate and upsell the differences in experiences available for VR vs. 360-video.

Hopefully Hollywood can learn from its 3D movie mistakes. James Cameron got the world to shift to digital projection to accommodate displaying *Avatar* at the highest quality possible, and ideally in 3D. When it came out in 2009, it took the world by storm for its (still) astounding visuals, and it remains the highest-grossing motion picture to date. Yet, rather than use the higher-end active shutter 3D glasses, many cinemas opted for the cheap polarized glasses.

When 3D HDTVs came out, the manufacturers cut corners by doing the same, and those TVs sadly died a quick death in the marketplace, as people became quickly disillusioned by the quality. Manufacturers must be quick to iterate their devices to something wireless, independent of a computer, and a lot less expensive.

Fortunately, the next iterations of VR headsets will be wireless and will not require a PC. Granted, the capability of this first version will not be as powerful as one linked to a workstation, but it might be a reasonable compromise if the cost stays low. Studies show the magic number for mass adoption is under $200, and Oculus Go hit that price point. So, we expect adoption rates to increase dramatically when Go hits the digital shelves, and for the power of these untethered headsets to increase to the level of high-end VR tethered headsets over the next couple of years.

## VR CREATIVE LANGUAGE

Some people fear that VR will replace the love that many have for films, even 3D films. But it is a different medium and a different creative language.

In fact, many who are masters of the 16x9 (widescreen) format, approach VR the same way, and it doesn't work. For example, directors cannot (well, should not) focus on a couple having a conversation at a bar and have nothing happen in the surrounding space, simply because the narrative requires it. Unless there is a specific plot-related reason the bar is empty, it should be full of extras that provide the scene its realistic ambience. Directors also need 3D audio or cues to make sure viewers focus on the conversation at the bar to drive the plot, and not get distracted by something else in the room. They also need to think about ways to direct attention around the full 360 experience visually (for example, by throwing a ball behind the user).

Those used to 16x9 would typically frame the dialogue with close-ups, two-shots, after an initial establishing shot. The point is, directors are used to cutting back and forth. Most people are told not to do this in 360, and the results are long stretches of dialogue that seem unnatural to modern audiences. This is especially true of action films that have rapid-fire editing, something in the neighborhood of 30 cuts with a Steadicam, just to show a character getting punched and thrown to the ground. VR Filmmakers don't (and shouldn't) shoot this way in 360. Some people cannot handle the handheld quick camera motions like those in Marvel films, because when replicated in VR, it often leads to motion sickness (even though they're never moving) due to visual vection, or the illusion of self-motion. Even the motion of walking can lead to a slightly upset stomach. That said, a lot of VR and 360-video directors have said that they've thrown out the rule book they followed even a few years ago as they experiment with the medium.

But, in general, the natural expression of VR is viewer exploration. This simply means that more thought needs to be given in the pre-production phase to make effective Cinematic VR. Special consideration is needed for set-building, which needs to be made to hide crew, lighting rigs, cables, shadows, and cameras that would normally be on the other side of a 2D camera, as the 360 camera sees all the way around it.

With VR/AR game engine or 6DoF playback, the story-telling gets more complicated as viewers enter rather than just witness the story. It is a true Point-Of-View (POV) experience. The film *Hardcore Henry* (2016) tried to recreate the same feeling in a narrative 2D movie form. But with VR and a programming script or AI, you can look a character directly in the eye and have it respond, which elevates the experience of immersion to a whole other level.

If you are concerned about scale beyond VR and 360-video platforms, it is technically feasible to produce content in the 360/VR format, and then to extract a traditional 16x9 version. This would allow an in-theater or TV movie Director's Cut release and an interactive experience at home. This in-home true-VR experience would permit an exponentially more engaging set of additional plotlines—offering owners of intellectual properties a distinct VR revenue generator beyond digital downloads and/or purchase of a Blu-Ray.

## VR STORYTELLING

VR requires a different approach to storytelling. Usually, in 2D, a director and their cinematographer work closely together to frame every shot the way they want you to see the story, and to control what you see, hear, and understand at any given point in the narrative. With 360/VR, the audience can look anywhere they wish. For those not used to constructing stories in this manner, it might feel like complete chaos.

It's useful first to discuss the concept of "story" and the concept of "storytelling," before we discuss the differences with VR content. According to a Chicago University study that placed 1,737 stories from Project Gutenberg into a computer, which analyzed the included language for their emotional content, the result was the discovery of only six core story arcs. Admittedly, this sample is small, only sorts fiction, and is only from the English language, but academic circles generally accept it. In no particular order, they are: rags to riches, riches to rags, tragedy, man in a hole (starting from a fall and rising), the rise-fall arc, the rise-fall-rise arc such as in Cinderella, and the fall-rise-fall arc as found in Shakespeare's Oedipus Rex.

Coincidentally, the latter two, slightly more complex arcs, are also the most popular, based on the sheer number of downloads over any other story kind. These stories seem to agree with author Kurt Vonnegut's thesis that stories have shapes (bit.ly/vonnegutvideo). If those are a bit too abstract, Christopher Booker outlined seven narratives as: overcoming the monster, rags to riches, the quest, voyage and return, comedy, tragedy, and rebirth.[46]

In other words, every book you ever read, any movie you ever watched, any story you were ever told, in one way or another, can be distilled to those structures if only looking at the bare bones assembly of it. This encapsulates nearly all human storytelling since the beginning of printed books. It would take 400 years before this was challenged, thanks to the development of a new technology for creating and consuming content.

Despite all this innovation over a century and a half, nothing fundamentally changed about storytelling. Now with VR, there is the introduction of "branching narratives" and the agency of the viewer/user to direct the story. This creates a fundamental shift in the entertainment and story-telling universe.

Now users can have a kind of free will in these environ-ments. There are a limited number of ways that a game story may branch before eventually returning to some part of an overall linear narrative that forces the game to a conclusion (of which there may be more than one). This is essentially like a modern 360 video version of the *Choose Your Own Adventure* or *Give Yourself Goosebumps* book series.

This example of a branching narrative is also another sticking point for the ROI of Cinematic VR. Most people have watched a film more than once. However, what if your favorite movies had branching narrative capabilities? It can be thought of as a VR extension of the multiple-storyline device used in films like *Love, Actually* (2003) and *Pulp Fiction* (1994), TV shows like *This is Us* (2016) and *Heroes* (2006-2010), and potentially the future of entertainment content.

It may be worth noting here that the movie *Clue* (1985) experimented with randomly assigning cinemas one of three different endings when the movie was released, and it was a spectacular failure. It was decades before the film gained traction as a cult classic, and part of that was that all versions of the ending were integrated into the movie for home viewing.

## BEING SOCIAL IN VR

One of the other remaining hurdles for VR is that, for the most part, it is still a singular experience. Most human beings are social creatures, and VR, by its very nature, is an isolating experience. Luckily, there is a company with nearly $1 billion USD in backing to make VR infinitely scalable at any resolution, for any device, while connecting users all over the planet via the cloud.

This is the genius behind Facebook Spaces, where anyone with an Oculus Rift or an HTC Vive can join friends from anywhere in the world, and share in a communal space. You can hear one another and even use video to see one another or their avatars in real-time. If we take this a step further, and enable legal streaming video on demand via Facebook (something it is actively negotiating), then friends from anywhere in the world could sit down to watch their favorite 2D, 3D, and VR movies together. In Spaces, friends and family could make choices as a group about the narrative VR selections, or talk and crack jokes in their private Spaces, without annoying other people the way it would in a traditional cinema.

Before we continue, it's best to be primed on the topic by watching this video from October 2016: bit.ly/videof8. Facebook CEO Mark Zuckerberg's excitement, at the F8 conference, is palpable.

Zuckerberg and his Facebook Spaces team show off all the current bells and whistles. What is absolutely critical to note in this demonstration is how it includes the ability to interact, control, and respond in real-time, to content and people outside of the Facebook Spaces at any moment. Not only does this feature hold important implications for the Internet of Things and Smart Devices, but the stroke of genius is to make something truly social. The immersion should be a continuum, and not a vacuum. Every other Social VR space blocks the user from intentionally accepting, let alone interacting with, whatever is outside of the virtual simulation.

For more examples of how Facebook Spaces is being used by brands, you can check out Slate's weekly live Facebook Spaces show.[47]

Facebook's user experience design is innovative and useful atop of being entertaining, while simultaneously it is non-disruptive to the marketplace. It does so by striving to be a natural extension of the continually evolving ecosystem everyone accepts as "Facebook," instead of a wild and steep learning curve most would not bother to learn. By being as frictionless as possible to adopt, Facebook has an almost insurmountable competitive advantage in the social VR space. If Facebook can pull off that feat (in much the same way it is stealing YouTube's traffic for video, content, and users), then it can convert those Facebook Spaces, users and content, into places where contextual ads can be placed for the benefit of your brands and your companies.

Besides the sales of the ads themselves, the amount of additional user information pouring from these Spaces will provide massive amounts of behavioral and statistical data. This will be invaluable not just to Facebook and its advertisers, but to enterprise, brands, and even governments. This data will also help to feed Facebook's continued development of complex neural networks, such as multiple AIs that oversee and automate many functions of Facebook's numerous algorithms.

The development of a space like this means the rapid evolution of marketing and advertising, *once again*. Rather than just pictures, text, and video, people will be able to look at, hear, pick up, spin, etc., three-dimensional objects of anything that is for sale. Different tier premiums will arise for ads, along with premiums based on where and when the advertisement can be placed. Furthermore, since Facebook knows so much about each individual watching content, the sponsorships, the ads, logo clothing, etc., can all be altered to cater to the preferences of each viewer on the fly, even if they are in a group. It's been suggested that the ads you see might even include yourself in the ad creative.

Most importantly, the video demonstrates Facebook, a social networking site in 2D, worked really hard and very fast at making a similarly compelling social virtual space; atop its current ecosystem and captive audience of 2 billion+ worldwide users.

No doubt, there will competitors in this market. There are already social VR mobile apps, and Facebook might run up against Snap in the VR space too. Or, given their current strategic advantage, Snap might beat Facebook in the AR space if purchased by or partnered with Google (using Project Tango/ARCore), as was rumored prior to Snap's IPO.[48] With Google's Daydream for VR, and Snap's magnetic attraction to 300 million+ users within a key demographic for VR/AR adopters, paired with Google's Search, YouTube, Ad Tech and advanced AI, they could be a formidable pairing.

*VIRTUAL & AUGMENTED EVENTS*

This same kind of group VR experience could be applied to a live or pre-recorded concert, one where millions of people who could not travel to see it or afford a ticket, can watch it together on their VR device. This was already demonstrated by Google.org (the philanthropic arm of Google) with their live Hamilton experience for 5,000 high school students across the country. Live Nation offers free concerts through the NextVR app, and the NBA is broadcasting games live in VR. AR can be used to enhance the live experience, overlaying useful video and relevant data during events.

VR and 360-video experiences have huge potential for entertainers and entertainment venues. Musicians and comedians already go directly to fans through their websites, driving additional revenue. In 2012, Louis C.K. offered a direct download of a comedy special and reportedly earned $4.5 million in less than 2 days (although admittedly his attempt at a direct-to-consumer series was less successful). Entertainment venues across the world can charge for entry into live events with front row seats and behind-the-scenes access to anyone in the world, like a supercharged version of a pay-per-view or premium TV event.

Now, add laser-focused programmatic advertising and retargeting thanks to Google, Facebook, Apple, etc. Multiply the number of times to display brands, logos, ads, etc., during set breaks, pre, mid, and post show, and the number of times people might opt to re-watch the show, and the chance to show the same or new kinds of ads all over again. A partnership with key musical artists with international appeal, like "Rihanna Live in 360" or "Celine

Dion Live from the Colosseum in Las Vegas," etc., would rake in exponential amounts of money for the tour/presentation that have hitherto been unable to be leveraged, but now can, thanks to VR.

For sports teams and venues, VR has already started to gain a foothold. Virtual Reality, and even 360-video, provides users the opportunity to watch their favorite sport(s) courtside at all key strategic points. That alone is enough to make most sign up for the premium of being able to watch the entire season in VR. No wonder the NBA and the NFL have jumped into VR. The Olympics in 2016 were shown in 360, and, with Intel replacing McDonalds as a major sponsor in 2018, we expect new technological advancements will be integrated into the February coverage.

AR is about to hit a tipping point for location-based applications that bring more engagement with fans, offering even more reason to physically go to venues. For example, Major League Baseball's app, demoed with the Apple iPhone 8 and X launch, allows fans within the stadium to get real-time information about the players and the game. And companies like Zeality are offering turnkey 360-video and AR solutions for sports teams and venues. In the very near future, sports and music fans will be using their phones for lights and photos, *and* to engage with whole new dimensions of the live experience (e.g. special AR animations for those with certain phones). That brings additional app revenue from in-app advertising. So event and venue Marketers need to think not only about getting people into seats, buying food and drinks, but also about what AR experiences accompany the program.

## THE ROLE OF SOCIAL MULTIPLAYER EXPERIENCES

Shared VR Experiences, known as "Social VR," are a relatively new concept. This is where multiple users are in the same place, having an interrelated experience. It's only a recent phenomenon because powering even one person in VR requires a lot of horsepower from any one machine. To ask a workstation to power two users has been up to this point rather difficult, if not impossible. Indeed, so far, most VR games are written for just one player.

The absence of the social aspect to VR, especially when compared to modern console and PC games, such as the MMORPG genre (Massively Multiplayer Online Role Playing Game), where there could be tens of thousands of players (or more) at any given time, from all around the world, is one of the key aspects missing for the mainstream adoption and success of VR.

Right now, there are location-based-experiences (LBE) for VR, such as The Void. These are akin to the laser tag arcades of the 1980's, only they have the capability to enable multi-player in the same environment(s). This is thanks to a considerable number of machines running the simulations at the arcade, with motion trackers for the players.

For instance, The Void was responsible for the Madame Tussaud's *Ghostbusters* VR experience in NYC. It is unfortunate to give VR yet another marketing catch-phrase like "hyper-reality," but the locations do include practical effects such as water misting, olfactory sensations (smells), wind/blast effects, and mechanical contraptions, along with a backpack that carries both the portable VR PC and haptic chest plate (that vibrates at certain frequencies when you get "hit"). You do not enter the experience alone; you can experience it with a friend(s). It's the latter that elevates this VR offering into a truly immersive location-based entertainment.

The Void is also unique because the interiors can be rearranged to suit a game, or a promotional event. Its walls and doors are just padded, modular pieces, which are overlaid with VR CGI per use case. Therefore, an apartment in NYC filled with ghosts can quite easily be textured with alternate graphics, and thus be converted into a Sci-Fi corridor *Alien* horror survival game. It is this flexibility and interactivity with the environment that has landed The Void a contract to make location based entertainment (LBE) inside Disney theme parks for their trial run at implementing VR. They have also partnered with Lucasfilm and ILMxLAB to bring a Star Wars-branded experience to Disney resorts.

At the moment, the solution to solving the issue of infinitely scalable users, along with visual and audio fidelity in VR, without huge latency, is being spearheaded by a company that initially received backing from Google. The London-based company is called, appropriately, Improbable.IO, and its unique selling proposition is called SpatialOS. Essentially, it stitches together multiple iterations of a game engine, such as Unity or Unreal, in a daisy-chained-cloud kind of environment.

Brands aren't restricted to creating combat experiences. For example, *Game of Thrones* could have a "Three Eyed Raven" experience where you embody a character that can see the past, present, and future (building on the success of their *Ascend The Wall* VR Event Experience), or even choose a point of view (POV) of many different characters within the show. It would be amazing to feel like you are flying on a dragon while your friend is fighting off white walkers. TV competition shows (e.g. *Chopped, Project Runway*) could create VR experiences where you and your friends can compete against a celebrity or against each other. There are a lot of consumers who would be eager to pay to feel like they are friends with celebrities—think of the revenue potential for something like "An Afternoon with Ryan Gosling" (with many variations of "Hey, girl") sponsored by California Tourism where Ryan shows you around Los Angeles. Or a "Lunch with Samuel L. Jackson" (with likely an R rating) with logical sponsors, great backdrops, and product placements. You could even sit in a party bus in a version of *Carpool Karaoke* where you have the opportunity to sing along with your favorite singers. The realism and interactivity in these environments would help increase length of tune, replaying of these experiences, and improve the brand value for the sponsorship investment. And they'd likely be additional revenue streams for the celebrities and intellectual property rights owners, and a lot of fun for consumers.

## VIRTUAL ECONOMY

Once these environments become more of a reality, powered by Amazon, Google, or Microsoft, these VR worlds can/will be massive virtual destinations capable of their own massive internal economies.

Indeed, something like this may prove to be one of the ways displaced workers of the near future make their living. If this sounds like we're simply daydreaming, be assured that there is actually some precedent. One simple example are all the new jobs created by social media, a phenomenon that just a decade ago did not exist.

Another precedent was launched in 2003 by Linden

Lab in San Francisco. The brainchild of Philip Rosedale, the simulation Second Life had over 1 million regular users by 2013. It had an independent economy worth an estimated $500 Million USD.[49] Of this, $60 Million USD had been cashed out by users, making the owner of avatar Anshe Chung its first virtual-to-real-world millionaire. (Even though they went through a rough patch during the summer of 2017, they are back up and running. Users still flock to its social VR worlds and to several of the social VR shows that have been launched within it.)

Thanks to ever-increasing broadband speeds, the possibility of creating an online space where game/VR users (utilizing their own machines), connected to a common portal, was an innovative idea whose time had come. While Second Life's roadmap did include a head-mounted-display (HMD), it was before its time and never materialized.

Also, to make Second Life more accessible to most people, the levels of detail capable were throttled to a point. This technical limitation thus permitted most users to travel within whatever spaces they were allowed to go in Second Life, without taxing their machines or the company's servers. However, this did cause the visual fidelity to plateau, and competitors have slowly siphoned off users.

Fast-forward just a few more years to 2016, and VR had finally hit the well-to-do early adopters and developer mainstream. Second Life is still, remarkably, around to this day. However, its founder stepped down in 2010. He re-emerged a few years later with High Fidelity, a new company to compete against the initial company and metaverse he founded.

High Fidelity is a social VR platform for users to create and deploy virtual worlds, and to explore and interact together in them. The software is free and open source.

While the technology for High Fidelity is still in Beta, it is intentionally created for whatever high-end VR device you may already have. Yet, those without a VR HMD can still enter the exact same virtual worlds of High Fidelity; they are just limited to using a flat monitor. The avatars and their worlds are considerably more detailed than Second Life.

Oddly, the videos on YouTube do not do the latest release any justice. The "public" spaces of High Fidelity are quite visually rich and permit many people to inhabit them at one time, in 4K quality, with real-time audio, video, and the ability to share such content. In "private" spaces operated and owned by the user(s)/Resident(s), the amount of detail added to an environment can be AAA game-engine quality; as much as their local machine can handle. It will be interesting to see what will ultimately be available and possible in the full release, especially as speeds increase in every part of the ecosystem, along with new delivery and compression technologies.

High Fidelity has further been trying to demonstrate these social aspects not just for entertainment, but also for work and enterprise. High Fidelity's most popular YouTube video demonstrates how to do a whiteboard session in their VR space, with one using an HTC VIVE and the other, an Oculus Rift: bit.ly/VRwhiteboard. The enterprise hasn't quite jumped all into social VR or VR for meetings, but as an alternative to travel or telepresence, it is a compelling substitute; just one that has yet to be explored fully.

Not surprisingly, the company that Philip Rosedale founded, Linden Lab, decided to begin its own entry into VR. Linden Lab has called this beta effort Project Sansar. This is a Hindi word that doesn't quite have a precise translation. This is likely fitting, since "Sansar" can mean things such as: earth, world, outside, and universe. All these words and their meanings are apt for the environment developments occurring within Project Sansar.

Linden Lab is unquestionably competing with High Fidelity, and they have visibly attempted to take the lessons of Second Life, and advance those previously throttled environments and their capabilities. Not only can "non-game creators" design, develop, and deploy their own worlds with spatial audio into social spaces, but Sansar also has its own store for assets, and an internal economy for ecommerce. It too intends to have virtual cinemas, auditoriums for concerts, meetings, and live events, classrooms, churches, museums, etc., where anyone can join, from anywhere in the world, at any time.

It's easy to dream that this kind of high-stakes ambition for a metaverse, perhaps if paired with the power of Improbable.io's SpatialOS, makes the cinematic fever dream of *The Matrix* look far less like science fiction. It looks substantially more like a scientific and artistic inevitability, given enough time, money, and dedication.

The present focus on development with Project Sansar is quite heavily reliant upon much higher-end, AAA-game-quality VR, having invited renowned game and visual effects artists to the alpha version of the software. The result has been the creation of incredibly detailed virtual reality worlds that are meant to be explored and savored for the attention to minutiae. Some worlds border on photorealism, and other worlds are hyper-realistic abstractions that are as wild and inventive as any dream or nightmare.

Is there room for both of these companies to do well? Might one end up dominating the other? It's difficult to tell, with many die-hard fans seemingly content to remain in Second Life (as many have spent a lot of time and real-world money to build their spaces and avatars). Whether any migrate to Project Sansar or to High Fidelity over time, especially as machines and VR gear become less costly and cumbersome, or they acquire new audiences of their own, time will tell soon enough. More than likely, the success of either metaverse will depend upon its flexibility to overlap with what is happening in the real world, whether it is physical, cultural, social, or economic.

An area of peculiar behavior in these simulations, not unlike that of most as we took baby steps into social media, was the way users seemed to organize in the virtual worlds vs. how they would in real life; even if they had never met the other users and never would. This had repercussions many could not have anticipated. A number of large and daring real world companies, such as IBM, Reuters, Pontiac, etc., created virtual offices in Second Life. Some even went so far as to advertise within it, thinking it the natural progression of print to the metaverse. They could not possibly have anticipated how very wrong they were.

Many users figuratively revolted in the virtual worlds against the advertising and corporate offices, defacing and destroying them *en masse*. Many users, known as Residents, went out of their way to not visit such spaces, even organizing others to do the same. Others would figure out ways to drive the poor souls who managed the corporate avatar(s) at any given shift slowly insane, often by being as incredibly profane and obscene as possible.

Users/Residents could be functionally anonymous. The repercussions for such behavior in Second Life were not the same as in the real world. Sadly, this worked against the greater good of Linden Labs, because without the investment of such advertising, sponsorship, and enterprise rent payments, continued development slowed to a crawl, limited expansion, culled their workforce, and restrained the innovative road-map the company had outlined.

Instead, Residents of Second Life set up their own mom-and-pop shops, selling all kinds of digital goods and services; such as avatar upgrades, packaging, and shipping physical goods. It was this kind of social interaction within an enclosed, virtual, and truly operational economy, with a sense of community, that kept users returning and paying their subscriptions.

The users also kept agreeing to the fees to put money into the digital economies of Second Life, as well as take it out, for the currency conversion equivalent to the real-world one(s) of their choice; after Linden Lab had taken a percentage for processing, like a credit card company. It was, therefore, possible to earn a living in the virtual world simulations of Second Life, and then bring those earnings into the real world. It was perhaps this development of social interaction in the virtual world that so amazed its creators and users, and stunned the financial world all at the time. For greater details on how this ended up working and thriving to this day, the book *The Making of Second Life: Notes from the New World*, by Wagner James Au, is a great chronicle of the beginnings of this metaverse.

It is doubtful the majority of those that enter into the future metaverse spaces would begin rioting at the mere display of advertising. Most people are used to the advertising that occurs all around them in real-life, as well as on the mobile web and in gaming apps. For example, in sports simulation types of AAA game titles, fans are already used to seeing ads on sports games on TV. It's a real-life reference to it that does not interrupt their psyche. In fact, a fake (or "mock") ad might draw more attention and distract from the realism of the experience. It's when advertising and marketing crosses beyond that currently accepted barrier, a personal space in the metaverse, that users become irate or "weirded out."

For example, it would not be acceptable for an expensive new high-rise in a metropolis, to have its pristine views of a sunset over the ocean disrupted by a similarly tall, flashing neon ad banner obstructing such a view. Something about a physically impossible structure, when mixed within real world parameters, is psychologically off-putting when people are spending vast numbers of hours in these worlds. Indeed, some people practically live in these worlds. They might even have literally mortgaged a virtual apartment, and the flashing neon might not only be a distraction, it could even be keeping the user avatars awake.

If such a flashing neon banner ad were to be erected in the real world, blocking spectacular ocean views, you can bet people would sue everyone responsible for the monstrosity, until it was removed, and they were remunerated. Therefore, it is likely best practice, at least for a time, that advertisers and marketers try to be respectful of similarities of life in VR, lest they turn off potential consumers.

## AUGMENTED SHOPPER MARKETING

In the past 20 years, the internet has dramatically changed shopping habits and patterns. Some people hardly go to the physical store anymore because they can shop online. The rapid evolution of e-commerce has set the tone for marketing, from mass retailers to online boutiques. Businesses understand that they can't grow if they do not have an online shopping cart available for their customers.

E-commerce is profitable and convenient for customers. However, it does not offer the opportunity for consumers to try on brand's products without leaving the comfort of their home. According to Augment, "The primary drawback to online shopping is that many of the sensory elements that customers use to make their purchasing decisions are often lost. When shopping online, a customer cannot touch or feel an item, see how it works, or know how it will fit in their home. The loss of this interactivity and presence in the shopping experience leads to uncertain buyers and more abandoned carts." That is why retail is becoming the next AR frontier.

AR is a tool for your companies to create an even more engaging and personal buying experience for your consumers. Even though customers are not physically in your store, they still need assistance and the best customer service. Research has shown consumer interest in AR shopping experiences:

- 71 percent of shoppers would shop at a retailer more often if they were offered AR.[50]

- 40 percent of shoppers would be more willing to pay more for a product if they could experience it through augmented reality.[51]

- 61 percent of shoppers prefer to shop at stores that offer AR, over ones that don't.[52]

We believe that brands can increase their customer conversions and decrease refunds by using AR because it provides customers with the chance to try on or virtually use the product and understand its features. It gives your brand(s) the opportunity to offer personalized shopping to your customers.

"This is the key to a new order. This code disk means freedom."

*Tron* (1982)

"And the world was more beautiful than I ever dreamed, but also more dangerous than I ever imagined."

Kevin Flynn, *Tron: Legacy* (2010)

Now that we have the tools of Augmented and Virtual Reality, it's important to not only dream of what we can do today or tomorrow, but to plan for the far future.

According to Tim Cook, Apple's CEO, "A significant portion of the population of developed countries, and eventually all countries, will have AR experiences every day, almost like eating three meals a day."[53] Google, Facebook, Apple, Microsoft, and many others are making the bet that VR/AR are the de-facto computation, entertainment, and social devices of the near future. But where does the technology go after the first 1-2 versions are released?

THE MOST DRAMATIC HARDWARE CHANGE IN THE coming years will be for AR. Right now, most people will experience AR via their smartphone. Technology futurists like Vito di Bari believe that eventually there won't be a smartphone. Users will begin manipulating items with their own two hands at any given interaction point (like in *Hyper-Reality* or in *Minority Report*). This allows you to look up and use both hands.

The device of the future will rest on your face. When headsets are fashionable, relatively inexpensive (under the "magic" $200 threshold), and tied to aspirational brands or celebrities, then public perception will change.

Even the iPhone 7 is 120x more powerful than the first iPhone, and that took less than 9 years. Although there is some debate about Moore's Law, which states that computational power doubles approximately every two years, the speed of innovation is still quite rapid. Within the next 10 years, the supercomputers that fit in our pockets could be miniaturized to sit comfortably on our faces all day, while retaining and expanding their current capabilities. When

ntum computing, cloud storage, and wireless
ined from 5G/6G+ and super-powered WiFi,
*Hyper-Reality* seems a lot less like fiction and
more like prophesy.

## VOLUMETRIC VIDEO

Although this distinction matters more to directors than
marketers, volumetric video is the ability to capture real 3-
Dimensions around objects. AT&T's Developer Blog
explains it well:

> "Though 360–degree video content can be very
> immersive and invoke a strong sense of presence, it
> restricts the viewer from moving in the scene.
> Viewers can look around in all directions, but they
> cannot move from the physical camera's position.
> Computer vision-based image processing and
> depth-sensing techniques can be used to capture
> scenes that a person can freely move within,
> overcoming the movement restrictions of current
> 360–degree video. Content produced using these
> techniques is often referred to as volumetric or
> free-viewpoint video. In volumetric video, the
> distance to every point in the scene is captured in
> addition to image data. Using this information, the
> 3D geometry of the scene can be reconstructed
> into a navigable space. If a boxing match were
> captured with a volumetric video system, a viewer
> could choose to enter the ring and view the fight as
> though they were the referee or one of the
> fighters."[54]

VR directors are excited about volumetric video capture because it will simplify shooting and make the difference between VR and AR less black and white and much more grey. Companies such as Uncorporeal, HypeVR, 8i, and DepthKit are on their way to making it possible. With volumetric capture and retina quality screens, a new, dynamic, creative world will be opened, forever changing the possibilities for visual storytellers everywhere.

## NO SCREENS!?!

Is VR the last screen? What happens when you're not wearing a VR headset? If you've ever seen *Blade Runner* or *Black Mirror*, then you can guess that visuals will be omnipresent via surfaces that are screens, holograms, and/or through smart contacts. While the latter may sound like science fiction, there are already multiple patents placed for such devices from the likes of Sony, Google, and Samsung.

"Wait a minute," you might say, "I don't want to be bombarded by ads all the time. I simply won't wear those contacts." Frankly, you may not have a choice in the matter. Anywhere you go, smart surfaces will project information into your line of sight and/or hearing. Why would a company like Google or Facebook, or even those who make traditional computers like Apple and Microsoft, continue to make such items when there ceases to be much of need or demand from the majority of the consuming public? Widescreen TVs, bulky workstations, or even thin and light laptops don't really have a place in a world where one device can replace and/or rule them all.

## VIRTUAL SPACES

Unlike AR, where you can still see the physical world, VR inserts you into another one. This offers tremendous opportunities for your product or service to "own" a world that's totally relevant to your brand.

Expanding on our earlier deep dive into Virtual Spaces, let us pretend there is a social space in VR that looks like a contemporary New York City bar. You sit down with your friends to talk and watch a sports game on a huge mock TV screen above the bartender. Market researchers will track that you prefer Corona, while your friend prefers Guinness. While you talk, the virtual bartender engages with you in a way perfected by AI's understanding of your mood and past behavior. The bartender might serve such beers in this space, as objects to hold for your avatars. Perhaps the beers are the cover charge to enter this virtual space with other strangers, since it is owned on virtual real estate. In this next virtual world, supported by new technology advancements, top brands can charge a premium for entry.

Continuing the bar scene example, there might be video of a sports game, whether live, pre-recorded, or completely artificial, and it would likely have sponsors as well as commercial breaks, but here is where it gets interesting. Even though you and your friend are in the same virtual space, and even if you are in the same physical room or on opposite sides of the planet, your unique preferences for a certain brand of beer will be shown as a commercial during the same commercial slot break. You will see and hear a different advertisement specifically tailored to your preferences.

Now, imagine that same level of advertising as you step out of the NYC bar into a virtual Times Square. All the ads on those massive screens, the billboards, the Broadway shows, the storefronts lining the streets, even the brands and logos on the clothes of the avatars that surround them, are all going to artificially accommodate to each user. In some virtual spaces, the changes might only be minor so as not to break the illusion of a shared world, but where possible, the virtual worlds will bend as much as possible to cater programmatically to you. If these are safe spaces where you can spend time with friends from all over the world, it's easy to imagine joining these virtual worlds in the future the way that for 20 years people would turn on the TV to tune into Must See TV.

## AR SEARCH MARKETING

As most companies know, search engine optimization (SEO) has become an essential part in any marketer's campaigns. SEO is all about organic reach. AR will impact SEO tremendously, meaning marketers and brands need to get on board and prepare for the AR tidal wave.

With AR, your potential customers will be able to walk on the street, pick up their mobile device or smart glasses and scan the street for information about what's surrounding them. According to *Search Engine Watch*, there are two types of AR: marker-based AR and marker-less AR. Marker-based augmented reality is when a specific object that is coded into an application triggers AR technology. It can be a sign or a well-known building in order to initiate AR interactions with the customer, such as pop-ups or promotions offered. Markerless augmented reality is triggered by patterns, colors, geolocation, but can also be initiated through search query or personalized parameters.

There are many things brands need to be aware of when making decisions to enter the AR realm:

- *Local Optimization:* Targeting the right audience in their respective locations.

- *Local Content*: Create relevant content, so your potential customers can engage with your ads.

- *Rankings*: Eventually brands will be ranked just like in SEO. This means "descriptive naming, alt-tagging, image dimensions and product angles, and image sitemaps will all become increasingly important to ensure accurate results for AR-based search."[55]

- *Reviews*: Customers will be leaving real-time reviews and pointers for fellow shoppers in the area. This will change the power dynamic between customers and retail locations even more than the start of websites like Yelp. AR will provide immediate feedback on how to meet your customer's needs and help build social trust for your brand.

- *Promotions*: You will be able to reel in potential shoppers nearby and increase your conversion rate.

- *Accuracy*: "Everything with respect to a restaurant's or store's location has to be 100% accurate, down to the exact geo-coordinates! Otherwise if there is any error, businesses will miss out of their chance to be accurately tracked by AR apps and hence will decrease their revenue."[56]

- *Consistency*: Cross-platform consistency will be crucial.

Most importantly, INVEST EARLY. Start on your AR SEO strategy right now, before the technology becomes mainstream and you fall behind.

## HOLOGRAMS

Let's briefly cover the topic of holograms. A true hologram is something that is projected into 3D space and has true volume, whether equal to the original or scaled up or down to suit the viewer. Ideally, such a true hologram would be in full color, solid (not semi-transparent), and properly synced to audio. Right now, a true holographic projection mechanism is still being worked on, but companies like 8i, Vntana, Ultrahaptics, and Kin-omo are working to usher in the next phase of holographic content.

While a lot is being done in the development of holography, it is a very long way from any kind of mainstream access for recording, reproduction, distribution, etc. For now, the closest thing to a hologram is something appearing through AR. A Star Trek-like holodeck where you can touch and feel a room full of holograms is still just science fiction, but it is on the roadmap for developers.

Remember, what seemed impossible two years ago is now possible.

## NEW REALITIES POWERED BY AI & MACHINE LEARNING

It has been suggested that we soon will enter immersive reality experiences that are not wholly a construct of human creativity. They might be an amalgam of human creativity peppered with artificial intelligence (AI). Multiple players will share their augmented selves and creativity, to constantly alter the parameters of a game or story in real-time. There also could be social AI with avatars that react to each user uniquely with emotions that make them seem human. AI can also help with the issues of depth of field for VR experiences, such as determining what a distant image might look like when users move up close. It may even be something developed entirely by an AI, so that we cannot even postulate what that could be. The way AI might *think* about story, structure, pacing, etc., could be entirely alien to us, and it could be the very novelty that draws us into it. An AI, knowing the limits of what humans understand as stories, might be able to develop something humans simply cannot conceive, and ultimately result in an immersive kind of storytelling unlike anything experienced to date. We might not even have a term for what such an experience might be, or for that matter, how it could affect us (the way that cinema or games can sometimes move us to emotional catharsis). Who knows, but we will soon find out.

## VR/AR & BLOCKCHAIN

As many know, beyond Bitcoin, blockchain technology is disrupting almost every industry, from finance, to real estate to law and also content and entertainment. While we have just started scratching the surface of what blockchain means for the future, blockchain can and will impact the VR/AR industry. Blockchain might serve as a repository for content and a way for VR and AR creators to get paid and credited for their content. An article from *The Coin Telegraph* mentions how startups like Cappasity are seeking to bridge the gap between creators and the need for 3D images that will increased radically with immersive content.[57] Blockchain can help solve the copyright issue that creators can face when their content is used without them being paid for it. Fred Ehrsam, co-founder of Coinbase, argues in a Medium post that actually VR is a Killer App for Blockchains.[58]

## IMPLANTS

Over the next few years, likely decades, we will witness VR, AR, and our physical world starting to blend and blur together into a continuum. VR/AR may soon be inseparable from our everyday lives, due to how embedded they are in our work, play, and interpersonal communications. What begins with smartphones gradually disappears and is ultimately replaced with smart-glasses, later with smart contacts, and more likely than not in the farther future, the option for implants. The conversation surrounding implants and human augmentation usually makes most people uncomfortable and would take a whole other book to discuss, so we only touch briefly on the subject matter.

By the time we are contemplating implants, we're likely considering a greater merger of our biology with technology that extends beyond VR, AR, and holograms. It is also likely to be a future where our minds can interface directly with the technology, and new kinds of content, along with different forms of consuming them.[59]

"The first rule of Fight Club, is you don't talk about Fight Club."

Tyler Durden in *Fight Club* (1999)

One of the hurdles facing people interested in VR/AR is that it feels almost like joining a club with a complicated initiation process. While there's a pretty open and collaborative community that is developing within the VR/AR industry, it's not as transparent as it could be. So, we wrote this section to help marketers jump in quickly and without anxiety.

ONE OF THE BIGGEST STRUGGLES WE'VE SEEN BETWEEN content creators and their clients is the question, "Does it need to be in VR?" or "Do we need AR?" This might seem like an odd question, especially as these companies need clients for their survival.

Influencer and ethnographer, Simon Sinek, studies what inspires people. One of the tools he uses is the idea of "Start with the Why," and it relates pretty directly to these questions.[60] Although Sinek wasn't specifically speaking about VR/AR, it's still important to answer the following questions before developing a VR or AR request for proposal (RFP) or creative brief:

- Why does my company want to create something in VR/AR?

- Why does this idea need to be in VR/AR?

Sinek continues on to offer some great marketing messaging advice: People buy the "why" and not the "what." Basically, there's a fundamental truth that comes out of this:

---

Not Everything Needs to Be In Virtual or Augmented Reality.

---

Isn't that counterproductive to put that in a book about Marketing for VR/AR?

Actually, no. Jeremy Bailenson, a professor of communication at Stanford University and the founder and director of its Virtual Human Interaction Lab, has a great tool for determining if something needs to be in VR:

## BAILENSON'S RULES FOR GOOD VR:[61]

- Expensive
- Dangerous
- Impossible
- Rare

Whether you agree or not with these rules, these rules help to frame the question of whether or not VR is the right marketing tool for your needs. If your customers can do it easily in real-life, there's likely no need to create a virtual one (until there's a virtual mall that recreates a real one). Bailenson also argues that VR should only be a 20-minute experience at most. There are more debates about the latter rule, but it's still worth mentioning.

For Augmented Reality, the rules of thumb haven't yet

been established, but we present some suggestions that we plan on updating as the industry matures:

- *Useful*: Does the AR technology make something simpler and easier than using the internet or looking in a book?

- *Integrated*: Does it make it feel like you've entered a new dimension of the real world?

- *Engaging*: Is there a reason to come back and use the AR tech again?

We would love to hear if you agree or disagree and others you would add.

## YOUR BRAND ENVIRONMENT OR SPACE

When you start to develop your brand, Brand Managers and Executives work together to identify their company's Brand Personality. The typical questions are: "Who would your brand be if it were a person?" "What would it be like?" "How would it act if it entered a room?" (And, no, not every brand can be The Rock, George Clooney, or Zendaya.) There's also a brand management process of identifying adjectives that define that personality, beyond product attributes. Through the Brand Personality answers, companies get a better sense of their brand and how to communicate consistently to their target customers.

For immersive experiences, we propose that this Personality question can become Brand Environment or Brand Space questions:

- If your brand were a place, what would it be like?

- What would you do there?

- What would you feel like when you are there?

- Would there be a lot of logos or not that many?

The answers to questions like these can help inform your creative brief and make sure that users have the right kind of experience.

"With great power there must also come great responsibility" (*Spider-Man,* 1962 comic book). Use your creative powers wisely when creating these new virtual worlds. You must consider your customer's experience in more detail than you ever have before. It is no wonder that Event Marketers and storytellers have embraced VR and AR. It's a similar set of questions that need to be answered before creative begins. Besides the standard questions about brand appropriateness and marketing goals, you should also consider the following questions:

- Is this experience something my target audience would want to do?

- What do I want my customer to feel? How does it make them feel about my brand?

- Will this experience change the way they experience my brand?

- Will this experience augment brand loyalty or increase engagement?

- How long do I want them to have this experience?

- How will there be a beginning, middle, and end of the experience? Are there multiple plotline choices along the way?

- Is there something they can share with their friends?

- What negative outcomes could arise from this experience?

- Could the consumers view this as gimmicky, or is it a genuine expression of the brand vision?

- Can users share their experiences socially?

Questions like these can help you think through the details of your VR/AR experience and not get distracted by the innovative technology.

## THE QUESTION OF RETENTION

Everyone in VR/AR has wondered about the "killer app" for VR and AR. What is going to bring in more than the early adopters to both mediums? We'd like to reframe the question about "killer apps" as having high retention levels.

Questions to ask yourself and your team are:

- What is going to keep users around longer?

- What's going to keep them coming back?

- How does VR/AR alter our customer's journey?

These are questions I'm sure you've asked yourself if you've managed a website or app. The same logic should not be lost when it comes to new technology. "But, it looks so cool!" isn't a retention strategy. VR and AR right now are bright, shiny objects, but your marketing fundamentals shouldn't go out the virtual window. Focus on what makes your product or service sticky, and increases the value of your company to investors, distributors, and/or advertisers.

## CREATIVE BRIEFS

In developing a VR/AR Marketing campaign, we recommend you write an overall marketing brief (i.e. an outline of everything in the campaign) to make sure everything is in one place and everyone is on the same page. As you may or may not know, typically a brief includes the history that led you to the creative, your goal, budget, timing, messaging, the expected media channels, purchase channels, the specific deliverables, expected promotion, and the research/ROI needed to prove the value of the campaign.

With VR/360-video/AR experiences specifically, there are some additional considerations that we recommend you include in your brief:

- *Reason for being in VR/AR*: Why is this the

right media for this execution? Can it be done as well in 2D or via a website?

- *Branching narratives* (*VR only*): For the multiple plotlines in VR, what multiple paths do you want users to take? Is there a beginning, middle, and end of the experience? How will the user choose the next step in the story (e.g. gaze activation)? (Expect a complicated wireframe to be created out of these questions.)

- *Emotion* (*VR/360-video only*): What do you want your viewers to feel during their experience?

- *Interactions* (*VR and MR*): Where do you want consumer interactions to take place within the experience? How is that related to the brand and the overall experience?

- *Triggers* (*AR only*): What specifically will trigger engagement with AR? Do you need to offer instructions to download something?

- *Deliverables*: Although included in every brief, be sure to be very specific in a VR/AR brief as there aren't standard specs. Outline which platforms and if there are different versions that need to be shot or built. Consider if it's going to be watched on a headset or on a flat screen. Also determine the Field of View you want for any 2D versions.

## VR/360-VIDEO PRODUCTION CONSIDERATIONS

As Marketers and communicators are still getting adjusted to these media, we felt it would be helpful to list some considerations when developing your campaigns. In general, we suggest you work with directors and production teams that already have experience in VR/360-video and ask to view their creative before signing any contract.

Here are some things we'd suggest that you discuss with your VR/360-video producer and director:

- *Audio*: Ideally you should record using spatial audio (vs. stereo or mono and converting). Figure out how to use sound to direct the viewer's attention.

- *Camera*: Shoot in 360 vs stitching together videos, if budgets allows. As the camera acts like a point-of-view (POV) shot, determine where the camera should be (e.g. sitting or standing, how tall the character is; don't put their head in the middle of a table after you established them as a person within the action) and how the user will interact with the rest of the product. Avoid moving the camera quickly as it may cause nausea, and avoid having an actor/host talk to the camera if the user can't talk back, unless that's key to the plot point (for example, a host guiding you shouldn't ask the user a question, if he/she can't talk back).

- *Cast*: Finding the right actors able to manage long takes (like theater actors) and yet be subtle (like film actors), as bad acting gets amplified in 360. Block your shots to make sure that the actors aren't constantly walking across seamlines.

- *Crew*: If shooting in 360, determine if the crew will be visible or if they will hide while the video is shooting.

- *Lighting*: Decide if you will be hiding the lighting apparatus during the production or editing it out in post-production.

- *Storyboard*: Map out what's going to happen in the experience in detail. Draw a storyboard on a cube map with each box representing roughly 90 degrees of the sphere and start to understand Jessica Brillhart's point of interest map, which she refers to as the "Hero's Journey."[62, 63] These will help you to identify ways to draw the attention of the user through audio, lighting, or moving objects. If it's true VR, you can identify story-appropriate ways to get the viewer to engage their whole bodies to kneel, walk through something, etc.

## ADDITIONAL TECHNICAL CONSIDERATIONS

- *Color & Exposure*: Make sure each eye matches if using stereoscopy.

- *Frame Rate*: At least 60 fps.

- *Latency*: As low as possible (ideally 0) to avoid nausea.

- *Seamlines*: Stitching is aligning the video to be one complete 360 video. Be aware of where the video footage connects as it sometime distorts or ghosts the people crossing it.

- *Synchronizing*: With so many pieces of the 360 puzzle, you need to make sure that each image and sound matches

Also, try a couple of shots where you break the rules, just in case it works. So many directors say that they are learning this medium as they are going.

## AR BRIEF CONSIDERATIONS

Once you are ready to jump into developing something in AR, here are some things to consider with your AR creative team:

- *App details*: Are you creating a new app or creating something to download in your existing app?

- *Call-to-action*: Where and how are you going to get potential users to start using your AR experience as seamlessly as possible?

- *Engagement*: How do you want users to use the graphics? How does it showcase the best of AR and deliver on your brand or marketing goals? How are you going to get users to re-engage?

- *Location*: Where are people going to use this AR experience? On their phone on the go? At home on their tablet? In a store? At an event? Can it go from one to another?

- *Shareability*: How easily can the AR experiences be shared socially?

- *Value*: What is the utility of the AR you're creating and how does it tie back to your brand promise? Or if it's just for fun, how does it bring value to your campaign as a whole?

## KEY PERFORMANCE INDICATORS (KPIs)

Before you launch marketing or branding campaigns, you need to determine what defines a success. As VR and AR are a relatively new media for marketers, case studies and marketing research are needed to support the value of your investment. A/B testing and engagement research will also identify your most enthusiastic users and how they are using and viewing your creative. We recommend partnering with a research firm like Retinad that specializes in VR/AR analytics.

Here are some sample research options:

- *Attitude*: As VR/360-video is an emotional

medium, it's important to know consumers' attitudes towards your brand before and after the VR/360-video experience. Attitudes may even improve after a highly engaging or useful AR experience.

- *Awareness*: Do people know about your brand yet? If so, what percentage of your target does? How does that change after the campaign?

- *Call-to-action*: What do you want people to do after they engage with your content? Track it as proof of the value of your campaign.

- *Engagement levels*: You need to track the details of what users are doing not only for improving the experience but also showcasing the value of the creative to partners. Similar to a website, these experiences can be measured with clicks, session length, OS, device type, ID, etc.

- *Heat mapping*: When you move your creative into a 360 environment, it's important to know where your consumers are gazing and for how long. It will show you if your users are following the journey you have laid out. This will be extremely important when you have integrated your products and brand into the creative.

- *New leads/lead conversions*: Did your VR/AR experience lead to more inquiries, sales, or donations?

- *Recall*: One of the selling points of VR/360-video is engagement, which should translate to whether consumers can remember your brand. Ideally, you should build in a brand recall test after the experience.

- *Social media/online data*: How many people typically visit your website and social media channels? How many after the campaign? How many people tweeted or shared about your experience?

- *Unique users/re-engagement*: 1) How many people used your experience, 2) How many people went back and used it again.

- *View through rate*: It's not just about whether people start your VR/360 experience, but also whether they finish it and where they might drop off. Not everyone is going to watch everything, but improving length of view/tune/use will show how effective and engaging your content is.

And, don't forget to make sharable videos of users engaging with your content enthusiastically for the first time. It will help show everyone how amazing your creative is, without *telling* your current and future clients how amazing it is.

## PUBLIC RELATIONS POSSIBILITIES

Augmented and Virtual Reality can amplify your company's media relations. Because VR and AR have not yet become commonplace, news about your organization embracing AR and VR can boost your brand. We used to send press kits, but soon we'll send journalists and bloggers branded, exclusive AR and VR content.

Augmented Reality allows for a lot of creativity for communications professionals. For example, AR digital video or 3D content can be overlaid on a press release, giving more dimensions than a press photo or 2D video. Axia Public Relations firm states that augmented reality "offers an inexpensive way to enhance content and increase the value of branding initiatives. It has become a popular way to leave breadcrumbs in strategic places, leading to a launch announcement or new product launch."[64]

Additionally, VR and AR will be an important element in employee training for crisis communications simulations. When Cathy worked in healthcare, they held crisis communications simulations every few months to ensure the communications team knew how to activate the crisis plan. Suppose you could experience crises before they happen. Would it change how your team prepares? VR can bring crisis-prep exercises from drills to full-blown simulations. It will enable PR pros to not only experience the crisis, but also deal with threats and weaknesses they might not have been ready for. VR will play a big part in corporate communications crisis plans and risk management.

VR and AR can also help amplify your media relations because members of the news media are leading the VR revolution by creating immersive content, including The New York Times' VR and the Huffington Post's Ryot

News. PR pros should learn from these media outlets. When you create immersive content, think like a journalist.

For April Fool's Day 2015, Atlanta's Daybook service posted a release titled "Daybook Announces New Holographic Press Release Service."[65] Of course, this was just a joke then, but in 2017, this is a reality. Cathy creates press releases with holograms and augmented reality content for brands. What seemed impossible two years ago is now possible.

The PR profession is about to change radically. Digital audiences have high expectations for how a brand should engage with them. The tactics that work today might not work tomorrow. Their palates evolved as they shifted how they engaged with digital content. VR and AR will be a new opportunity for brands to interact with consumers in an entirely different way from traditional methods. AR will start solving businesses pain points; it will facilitate our lives and provide us with real-time data that we need. Brands, PR agencies, and PR pros need to stop seeing AR as tomorrow's trend and start embracing it today. The tech of tomorrow is already here. Just look at what PR agencies like Ketchum and MSLGroup are doing. Ketchum launched a VR specialty group at the Cannes Lions and has already worked with Samsung Electronics and Clorox Healthcare.[66] Their VR agency employs 40 technology, video, entertainment-event and user-experience experts and has formed partnerships with VR leaders. MSLGroup has been also been venturing into VR.[67]

Marketing, Branding, and Public Relations professionals have the chance to take their industries to new heights (or new "dimensions") with AR and VR. As the VR/AR industry is growing quickly, Marketers and communicators don't have to have a narrow definition of their role within it.

We say: dive in. Test the latest gear. Create content and design VR environments. Develop an AR app. Craft immersive stories and strategies for your companies and your clients. Lead your companies into the future with VR and AR. Share the marketing potential, the engagement benefits, the case studies, the opportunity cost of not doing anything. Forward-thinking companies, not just the social media behemoths, are tapping into this amazing opportunity.

Marketing, branding, and PR professionals can use augmented and virtual reality in a variety of ways across the customer's decision-making journey:

## 1. BUILD AWARENESS & FAMILIARITY

Companies implementing VR/AR invite press coverage and word-of-mouth.

## 2. ENABLE ENGAGEMENT & EVALUATION

Bring your product/service to life. Customers engage not only because of what's being promoted, but because they have the chance to interact with your product in a new and different way.

## 3. CREATE AN EMOTIONAL CONNECTION

VR and AR are great conduits for empathy and, in turn, action. "On a lifetime value basis, emotionally connected customers are more than twice as valuable as highly satisfied customers."[68]

## 4. TAKE ADVANTAGE OF THE MEDIUM

Bring consumers to places they cannot go; make the impossible possible. Use VR and AR in ways no one has tried before. Showcase that your brand is not only modern but innovative, useful, and customer-focused.

## 5. DIVE INTO THE FUTURE OF PRODUCT SAMPLING

In a pre-internet world, product sampling was one of the best marketing methods to drive purchase. AR and VR will usher in a new renaissance of product sampling. We expect these interactive and useful tools to decrease the time from consideration to purchase, as users can put products in their own world (with AR) or more easily imagine themselves using the product (with VR and AR).

## 6. TIE YOUR ACTIVATIONS TO CALL-TO-ACTIONS

When possible and natural, allow for simple post-interaction purchase or action. Not only does it drive business, but it will be an easy KPI.

## 7. TURN MORE CONSUMERS INTO BRAND ADVOCATES

VR and AR will create a stronger relationship between companies and consumers. If you get your advertising and messaging right, your customers will drive word-of-mouth and/or be more likely to activate your call-to-action.

## 8. GROW CUSTOMER LOYALTY

Immersive content builds consumer loyalty and is powerful for brands that know what they stand for and how to communicate it. VR and AR reinforces loyal customers, while funneling and converting new ones.

## 9. COMMIT TO THE INVESTMENT

VR and AR shouldn't be a one-and-done type of investment. For example, "[b]eauty brands are constantly faced with the challenge of creating a connection between physical products and customers," said James McCrae, Head of Digital Strategy at Blue Fountain Media. "However, brands should only commit to something like AR if they're going to keep investing." If you have a customer that expects the newest technology, not keeping up your end of the bargain breaks your brand promise and creates the opportunity to lose brand loyalty.

*10. HAVE FUN!*

ONE OF THE SCIENCE FICTION GREATS, ARTHUR C. Clarke, said that, "Any sufficiently advanced technology is indistinguishable from magic."[69] Virtual reality and augmented reality demonstrate Marketing and communications tools we never thought possible. Even the low-tech AR experience of Pokémon Go would seem like something from a science fiction movie, just five years ago. The technology and processing power has reached a tipping point, and we aren't looking back.

Steve Jobs said, "Innovation distinguishes between a leader and a follower."[70] CEOs, CMOs, and their employees need to cut through the hype or backlash of new products and services to see what will work with their companies. Although not all companies define themselves by their use of innovative marketing tools, it is important to prepare for the future and not be left behind.

The next couple of years will be exciting for Marketers, brands, programmers, technologists, and general consumers. There is sure to be a lot of innovation, but VR/AR companies need Marketers and communicators like you to push the medium forward. On the one hand, users have downloaded over 300 million apps for VR, which was 56% of all downloads in 2017 (the second closest category was Entertainment, at 17%).[71] Yet, most people experiencing VR are doing so via mobile experiences that don't enable room-scale effects or 6DoF. Thus, the majority of the world's exposure to VR has really been 360-video, which many say is really just "2D 360 video." Marketers and PR professionals have the ability to grow the user base and showcase the value of true VR, increasing the rate of adoption and the diversity of experiences.

Apple's new phone launch promises that AR will go truly mainstream, even though AR is much further behind developmentally than VR. AR can still be very useful across a considerably wide swath of older phones with a free iOS update, at no extra cost to the consumer. Not counting iPads or iPhone 8 and X sales, that's conservatively an audience of greater than 250 million users worldwide, who have an iPhone 5S and above. VR doesn't have the same access, because you can't get VR with a simple iOS update. You must take charge and help to create amazing user experiences that change and improve upon current technologies.

With your help, these technologies will be even more accessible to consumers. With the loss of tether (expected by the publishing of this book), the release of VR tech that permits telling the same 6-7 stories, and the ultimate ubiquity of the new iPhone and its related technology, VR and AR will be part of our everyday living. It will help us have new and exciting experiences, feel like we've travel to places we've never even imagined, find our way more easily in stores, help us decide what drinks to have at Starbucks, let us know if there are exceptional experiences within walking distance, and allow use to virtually compare one product to another in new and more engaging ways. It's simply put, a revolution of marketing, branding, and communications. And, it's a digital wave that we can't wait to ride, and we hope this book allows you to join us.

*"Going outside is highly overrated."*

*Anorak's Almanac* in Ready Player One

When talking about VR and AR, most people tend to use entertainment references. Why? Because these technologies are unlike what has been experienced in real life. The following are some of the most frequently referenced pop culture VR and AR applications. Think of it as a fun list of required reading and viewing:

MOVIES

- *Blade Runner* (1982, Ridley Scott) & *Blade Runner 2049* (Oct 2017, Denis Villeneuve)

- *Fight Club* (1999, David Fincher)

- *Inception* (2010, Christopher Nolan)

- *The Lawnmower Man* (1992, Brett Leonard)

- *Disclosure* (1994, Barry Levinson)

- *The Matrix* (1999, The Wachowskis)

- *Minority Report* (2002, Steven Spielberg)

- *Ghost in the Shell* (2017, Rupert Sanders)

- *Ready Player One* (2018, Steven Spielberg)

- *Star Wars* series

- *Strange Days* (1995, Kathryn Bigelow)

- *Total Recall* (1990, Paul Verhoeven)

- *Tron* (1982, Steven Lisberger) & *Tron Legacy* (2010, Joseph Kosinski)

## TELEVISION

*Black Mirror* (Britain's Channel 4, Netflix):

- "The Entire History of You" (Season 1, Episode 3)

- "Be Right Back" (Season 2, Episode 1)

- "Playtest" (Season 3, Episode 2)

- "San Junipero" (Season 3, Episode 4)

*Futurama*

- "The Series Has Landed" (Season 1, Episode 2)

- "The Byciclops Built for Two" (Season 2, Episode 13)

- "Parasites Lost" (Season 3, Episode 4)

- "I Dated A Robot" (Season 3, Episode 15)

- "Near-Death Wish" (Season 7, Episode 10)

*Mr. Robot* (USA)
*Murder, She Wrote*

- "A Virtual Murder" (Season 10, Episode 5)

*Star Trek* (multiple series)
*Westworld* (HBO)

## BOOKS

- *Fahrenheit 451* (1953, Ray Bradbury)

- *Neuromancer* (1984, William Gibson)

- *Ready Player One* (2011, Ernest Cline)

- *Snowcrash* (1992, Neal Stephenson)

## IMMERSIVE THEATER & EXPERIENCES

- Escape Rooms (various)

- *Sleep No More*

- *Jump Into The Light*

- *Then She Fell*

1. Loiperdinger, Martin, and Bernd Elzer. "Lumiere's Arrival of the Train: Cinema's Founding Myth." The Moving Image. July 26, 2004. Accessed October 28, 2017. https://muse.jhu.edu/article/171125.

2. Hollerer, Tobias, and Dieter Schmalstieg. "Informit." A Brief History of Augmented Reality | InformIT. June 10, 2016. Accessed October 25, 2017. http://www.informit.com/articles/article.aspx?p=2516729&seqNum=2.

3. Minotti, Mike. "Pokémon Go passes $1.2 billion in revenue and 752 million downloads." VentureBeat. June 30, 2017. Accessed October 25, 2017. https://venturebeat.com/2017/06/30/pokemon-go-passes-1-2-billion-in-revenue-and-752-million-downloads/.

4. Chen, Eden. "How Augmented Reality Will Shape the Future of Ecommerce." Entrepreneur. January 16, 2017. Accessed October 25, 2017. https://www.entrepreneur.com/article/287687.

5. Castellanos, Sara. "What Is a Hologram?" The Wall Street Journal. December 12, 2016. Accessed October 25, 2017. https://www.wsj.com/articles/what-is-a-hologram-1481551200.

6. Damiani, Jesse. "Facebook Brings More VR to News Feed With '3D Posts'." VRScout. October 11, 2017. Accessed October 25, 2017. https://vrscout.com/news/facebook-vr-news-feed-3d-posts/.

7. Mueller, Corey. "Google Lets You Listen To 3D Virtual Reality Audio In Your Headphones." Popular Science. July 25, 2016. Accessed October 25, 2017. https://www.popsci.-com/google-gives-new-spatial-vr-audio-omnitone#page-2.

8. Lalwani, Mona. "Surrounded by sound: how 3D audio hacks your brain." The Verge. February 12, 2015. Accessed October 25, 2017. https://www.theverge.-com/2015/2/12/8021733/3d-audio-3dio-binaural-immer-sive-vr-sound-times-square-new-york.

9. Vanian, Jonathan. "Google Has Shipped Millions of Cardboard Virtual Reality Devices." Fortune. Accessed October 25, 2017. http://fortune.com/2017/03/01/google-cardboard-virtual-reality-shipments/.

10. Mirt, Jernej. "Virtual Reality HMDs 2016 Sales Numbers." Custom Branded VR Cardboards | ViarBox. January 20, 2017. Accessed October 25, 2017. https://www.viarbox.com/single-post/2017/01/20/Vir-tual-Reality-HMDs-2016-Sales-Numbers.

11. Lunden, Ingrid. "Google has shipped 10M Cardboard VR viewers, 160M Cardboard app downloads." TechCrunch. February 28, 2017. Accessed October 25, 2017. https://techcrunch.com/2017/02/28/google-has-shipped-10m-cardboard-vr-viewers-160m-cardboard-app-downloads/.

12, 13, 14, 15. Goldstein, Andrew. "Re-Thinking VR Market Adoption in 2017." VRScout. July 24, 2017. Accessed October 25, 2017. https://vrscout.com/news/vr-market-adoption-2017/.

16. Terdiman, Daniel. "VR and Augmented Reality Will Soon Be Worth $150 Billion. Here Are The Major Players." Fast Company. November 25, 2015. Accessed October 25, 2017. http://www.fastcompany.com/3052209/tech-forecast/vr-and-augmented-reality-will-soon-be-worth-150-billion-here-are-the-major-pla.

17. "After mixed year, mobile AR to drive $108 billion VR/AR market by 2021." NEWS DigiCapital After mixed year mobile AR to drive 108 billion VRAR market by 2021 Comments. January 2017. Accessed October 25, 2017. https://www.digi-capital.com/news/2017/01/after-mixed-year-mobile-ar-to-drive-108-billion-vrar-market-by-2021/#.WfFb-WhSzIV.

18. "Global Games-Everything You Need to Know about 2017 So Far." SuperData Research. Accessed October 25, 2017. https://superdata-research.myshopify.com/products/year-in-review.

19. "Worldwide Revenues for Augmented and Virtual Reality Forecast to Reach $162 Billion in 2020, According to IDC." Www.idc.com. August 15, 2016. Accessed October 25, 2017. https://www.idc.com/getdoc.jsp?containerId=prUS41676216.

20. Virtual & Augmented Reality: Understanding the Race for the Next Computing Platform. Report. Goldman Sachs, Equity Research. January 13, 2016. Accessed October 25, 2017. http://www.goldmansachs.com/our-thinking/pages/technology-driving-innovation-folder/virtual-and-augmented-reality/report.pdf.

21. "Facebook ad revenue 2009-2016." Statista. 2017. Accessed October 26, 2017. https://www.statista.com/statistics/271258/facebooks-advertising-revenue-worldwide/.

22. "Google: ad revenue 2001-2016." Statista. 2017. Accessed October 26, 2017. https://www.statista.com/statistics/266249/advertising-revenue-of-google/.

23. Price, Rob. "The 2 key reasons behind the $1.1 billion Google-HTC smartphone deal." Business Insider. September 21, 2017. Accessed October 26, 2017. http://www.businessinsider.com/why-google-paid-1-1-billion-htc-pixel-team-2017-9.

24. Mohan, Pavithra. "Snapchat CEO: Our dancing hot dog is." Fast Company. August 10, 2017. Accessed October 26, 2017. https://www.fastcompany.com/40452199/snapchat-ceo-our-dancing-hot-dog-is-the-worlds-first-augmented-reality-superstar.

25. Marvin, Ginny. "USA Today Network's VR ad studio head: We've shown there's an audience for VR ads." Marketing Land. October 02, 2017. Accessed October 26, 2017. https://marketingland.com/usa-today-networks-vr-ad-studio-head-weve-shown-theres-audience-vr-ads-225207.

26. Liptak, Andrew. "There Are Some Super Shady Things in Oculus Rift's Terms of Service (Updated)." Gizmodo. April 02, 2016. Accessed October 26, 2017. https://gizmo-do.com/there-are-some-super-shady-things-in-oculus-rifts-terms-1768678169.

27. "Press Release: Airpush Partners with Nielsen and Three Leading Brands, Releases the World's First Virtual Reality Ad Effectiveness Study." VirtualSKY. December 8, 2016. Accessed October 26, 2017. https://virtualsky.-com/news-and-press/press-release-airpush-partners-nielsen-three-leading-brands-releases-worlds-first-virtual-reality-ad-effectiveness-study/.

28. Johnson, Lauren. "Buoyed by the Success of the Dancing Hot Dog, Snapchat Is Opening Up 3-D AR Ads for the Real World." Adweek. September 28, 2017. Accessed October 28, 2017. http://www.adweek.com/digi-tal/buoyed-by-the-success-of-the-dancing-hot-dog-snapchat-is-opening-up-3d-ar-ads-for-the-real-world/.

29, 30. "Groundbreaking Virtual Reality Research Show-cases Strong Emotional Engagement for Brands, According to YuMe and Nielsen." YuMe.com. November 09, 2016. Accessed October 26, 2017. http://www.yume.-

com/news/press-releases/groundbreaking-virtual-reality-research-showcases-strong-emotional-engagement.

31. Leemon, Daniel and Alan Zorfas. "An Emotional Connection Matters More than Customer Satisfaction." Harvard Business Review. April 24, 2017. Accessed October 26, 2017. https://hbr.org/2016/08/an-emotional-connection-matters-more-than-customer-satisfaction.

32. Everts, Tammy. "53% of mobile users abandon sites that take longer than 3 seconds to load." SOASTA. September 14, 2016. Accessed October 26, 2017. https://www.soasta.com/blog/google-mobile-web-performance-study/.

33. Singletary, Charles. "Facebook Social Experiment Reveals Introverts Open Up In VR." UploadVR. January 12, 2017. Accessed October 26, 2017. https://uploadvr.com/social-vr-facebook-engagement/.

34. Kokalitcheva, Kia. "U.S. Adults Are All About Their Smartphones and Online Video Streaming." Fortune. June 27, 2016. Accessed October 28, 2017. http://fortune.com/2016/06/27/nielsen-2016-q1-report/.

35. Javornik, Ana. "What Marketers Need to Understand About Augmented Reality." Harvard Business Review. April 18, 2016. Accessed October 26, 2017. https://hbr.org/2016/04/what-marketers-need-to-understand-about-augmented-reality.

36. Samit, Jay. "Augmented Reality: Marketing's Trillion-Dollar Opportunity." Ad Age. July 18, 2017. Accessed

October 28, 2017. http://adage.com/article/deloitte-digi-tal/augmented-reality-marketing-s-trillion-dollar-opportu-nity/309678/.

37. Richards, Katie. "Why More Brands Aren't Making Quality Virtual Reality and Augmented Reality Experiences." Adweek. January 06, 2017. Accessed October 28, 2017. http://www.adweek.com/digital/why-more-brands-arent-making-quality-virtual-reality-and-augmented-reality-experiences-175392/.

38. Martin, Chuck. "AR Marketing Shifting, $13 Billion Ad Revenue Projected." 04/24/2017. April 24, 2017. Accessed October 26, 2017. https://www.mediapost.-com/publications/article/299593/ar-marketing-shifting-13-billion-ad-revenue-proj.html.

39. Martin, Chuck. "AR Marketing Shifting, $13 Billion Ad Revenue Projected." MediaPost. April 24, 2017. Accessed October 28, 2017. https://www.mediapost.com/publica-tions/article/299593/ar-marketing-shifting-13-billion-ad-revenue-proj.html.

40. Mangiaforte, Lauren. "Why Augmented Reality Marketing Will Be Huge in 2015." Business 2 Community. December 03, 2014. Accessed October 26, 2017. http://www.business2community.com/brandviews/news-cred/augmented-reality-marketing-will-huge-2015-01086301#4OwxSviASYFV7X6O.97.

41. Samit, Jay. "Augmented Reality: Marketing's Trillion-Dollar Opportunity." Ad Age. July 18, 2017. Accessed October 26, 2017. http://adage.com/article/deloitte-digi-

tal/augmented-reality-marketing-s-trillion-dollar-opportu-
nity/309678/.

42. Meriwether, Cortney. "Augmented Reality: Altering the
Future of Marketing." Content. April 18, 2017. Accessed
October 26, 2017. http://contentplus.paceco.com/emerg-
ing-technology/augmented-reality-future-tech/.

43. Forbes Agency Council. "11 Creative Uses Of
Augmented Reality In Marketing And Advertising." Forbes.
June 13, 2017. Accessed October 26, 2017. https://www.-
forbes.com/sites/forbesagencycouncil/2017/06/13/11-
creative-uses-of-augmented-reality-in-marketing-and-adver-
tising/2/#35b49d552e33.

44. Mangiaforte, Lauren. "Why Augmented Reality
Marketing Will Be Huge in 2015." Business 2 Community.
December 03, 2014. Accessed October 26, 2017.
http://www.business2community.com/brandviews/news-
cred/augmented-reality-marketing-will-huge-2015-
01086301#FUpVIS6uK8g4OZiO.97.

45. Curtin, Keith. "Brands will soon score big with mixed
reality." Brands betting on augmented reality | The
Network | The Network. September 18, 2017. Accessed
October 26, 2017. https://newsroom.cisco.com/feature-
content?type=webcontent&articleId=1878311

46. "The Seven Basic Plots." Wikipedia. October 25, 2017.
Accessed October 28, 2017.
https://en.wikipedia.org/wiki/The_Seven_Basic_Plots.

47. Roettgers, Janko. "Slate Launches Weekly Facebook Live Talk Show Produced in Virtual Reality (EXCLUSIVE)." Variety. July 13, 2017. Accessed October 28, 2017. http://variety.com/2017/digital/news/slate-conundrums-facebook-live-vr-1202493894/.

48. Constine, Josh. "Google reportedly offered $30 billion to acquire Snapchat." TechCrunch. August 03, 2017. Accessed October 28, 2017. https://techcrunch.-com/2017/08/03/google-buy-snap/.

49. Maiberg, Emanuel. "Why Is 'Second Life' Still a Thing?" Motherboard. April 29, 2016. Accessed October 28, 2017. https://motherboard.vice.com/en_us/article/z43mwj/why-is-second-life-still-a-thing-gaming-virtual-reality.

50, 51, 52. Lunka, Ryan. "Retail Data: 100 Stats About Retail, eCommerce & Digital Marketing." Retail Data 100 Stats About Retail eCommerce Digital Marketing Comments. May 10, 2016. Accessed October 26, 2017. https://www.nchannel.com/blog/retail-data-ecommerce-statistics/.

53. Raymundo, Oscar. "Tim Cook: Augmented reality will be an essential part of your daily life, like the iPhone." Macworld. October 03, 2016. Accessed October 28, 2017. https://www.macworld.com/article/3126607/ios/tim-cook-augmented-reality-will-be-an-essential-part-of-your-daily-life-like-the-iphone.html.

54. Morton, Andrea. "Exploring Video Formats to Create VR/AR." AT&T Developer. July 13, 2016. Accessed

October 26, 2017. https://developer.att.com/blog/shape-future-of-video.

55. Pasqua, Rachel. "Augmented Reality & SEO: Search in an Annotated World." Search Engine Watch. July 05, 2013. Accessed October 26, 2017. https://searchenginewatch.com/sew/opinion/2279337/augmented-reality-seo-search-in-an-annotated-world.

56. "Direct Agents." Direct Agents. Accessed October 28, 2017. https://www.directagents.com/.

57. Buck, Jon. "VR Needs Blockchain to Solve Copyright Issues: Interview with Cappasity Founder." Cointelegraph. August 29, 2017. Accessed October 26, 2017. https://cointelegraph.com/news/vr-needs-blockchain-to-solve-copyright-issues-interview-with-cappasity-founder.

58. Ehrsam, Fred. "VR is a Killer App for Blockchains – Fred Ehrsam – Medium." Medium. February 13, 2017. Accessed October 26, 2017. https://medium.com/@FEhrsam/vr-is-a-killer-blockchain-app-3a4122d7f505.

59. Constine, Josh. "Facebook is building brain-computer interfaces for typing and skin-hearing." TechCrunch. April 19, 2017. Accessed October 28, 2017. https://techcrunch.com/2017/04/19/facebook-brain-interface/.

60. Start With Why. Accessed October 28, 2017. https://startwithwhy.com/.

61. Oremus, Will. "There Are Only Four Good Reasons to Do Virtual Reality." Slate Magazine. August 11, 2016. Accessed October 28, 2017. http://www.slate.com/articles/technology/future_tense/2016/08/the_only_good_reasons_to_use_virtual_reality_and_the_current_vr_renaissance.html.

62. Kuzyakov, Evgeny, and David Pio. "Under the hood: Building 360 video." Facebook Code. October 15, 2015. Accessed October 26, 2017. https://code.facebook.com/posts/1638767863078802/under-the-hood-building-360-video/.

63. Brillhart, Jessica. "The Language of VR – Medium." Medium. Accessed October 26, 2017. https://medium.com/the-language-of-vr.

64. Underwood, Darby. "How Augmented Reality can be used in PR in ways you never thought possible." Axia Public Relations. March 28, 2014. Accessed October 26, 2017. http://www.axiapr.com/blog/augmented-reality-can-used-pr-w.

65. "Daybook Announces New Holographic Press Release Service." Atlanta Daybook. Accessed October 28, 2017. https://atlanta.daybooknetwork.com/story/2015-04-05/50427-daybook-new-holographic-servic/.

66. Czarnecki, Sean. "Ketchum makes VR specialty group a reality." PR Week. Accessed October 28, 2017. https://www.prweek.com/article/1400173/ketchum-makes-vr-specialty-group-reality.

67. "Let's Break Tradition." Virtual Reality in Public Relations. Accessed October 28, 2017. http://vr.mslgroup.com/.

68. Zorfas, Alan, and Daniel Leemon. "An Emotional Connection Matters More than Customer Satisfaction." Harvard Business Review. April 24, 2017. Accessed October 26, 2017. https://hbr.org/2016/08/an-emotional-connection-matters-more-than-customer-satisfaction.

69. "Sir Arthur's Quotations." The Arthur C. Clarke Foundation. Accessed October 28, 2017. https://www.clarke-foundation.org/about-sir-arthur/sir-arthurs-quotations/.

70. Griggs, Brandon. "10 great quotes from Steve Jobs." CNN. January 04, 2016. Accessed October 28, 2017. http://www.cnn.com/2012/10/04/tech/innovation/steve-jobs-quotes/index.html.

71. Intelligence, BI. "VR app downloads skyrocket in 2016." Business Insider. April 13, 2017. Accessed October 28, 2017. http://www.businessinsider.com/vr-app-downloads-skyrocket-in-2016-2017-4?r=UK&IR=T.

*CATHY HACKL*

Cathy Hackl is an Emmy-nominated communicator turned Marketing Futurist, Latina tech leader and sought-after technology speaker. She's the co-chair of the VRAR Association's Marketing Committee and one of the top women in the VR/AR space. She served as Chief Communications & Content Officer for Future Lighthouse, one of the world's top VR studios focused on branded VR narrative, where she collaborated on projects with brands like Sony Pictures Entertainment, Oculus, Beefeater, and William Morris Endeavor. Hackl writes an emerging tech monthly column for the Public Relations Society of America's Tactics publication and is the VR/AR Evangelist for Changeville Arts in Music Festival.

Hackl was also selected as a 2017 Oculus Launch Pad Fellow, a program designed to support promising diverse VR content creators and help them bring their unique ideas to market. She currently helps innovative tech brands with highly specialized communications services, while teaching communicators about the latest tools and tech. She's also the founder of Latinos in VR/AR and one of the women leading the virtual revolution. Cathy was named by Onalytica and IZEA as a leading augmented reality and virtual reality influencer and also by NBC News as one of the top Latina women working in virtual reality.

Hackl has taught professional development workshops for the Public Relations Society of America and has participated in VR/AR Marketing webinars for VentureBeat. She's a sought-after VR/AR PR pro, who can translate tech speak to plain speak. Hackl was asked by Social Media Examiner's Social Media Marketing Society to lead a VR/AR marketing training for its members in June 2017.

Fluent in English, Spanish and Portuguese, she has spoken about VR and social media in more than 10 countries and has been invited to speak at Twitter's HQ in San Francisco, Facebook's HQ in Menlo Park, and at Sony's HQ in San Diego. Cathy has been featured in media outlets like Mic, CNN, Entrepreneur, VentureBeat, and Mashable. Hackl is also the co-chair of the VR/AR Association's Marketing Committee and a leading voice in the VR/AR marketing space.

Before working in AR, VR and social media, she worked as a journalist for CNN, Discovery Communications, and ABC News. Hackl has a BA in Broadcast Journalism from the University of Texas at Austin and a double Masters in Mass Communication and Latin American and Caribbean Studies from Florida International University. She has taught at IE Business in Madrid and at SDA Bocconi in Milan, two of Europe's top business schools. In 2015, she obtained her APR (Accreditation in Public Relations), a highly-specialized and respected accreditation in the communications industry. She teaches professional development classes for the Public Relations Society of America and is an emerging tech columnist for PRSA's Tactics publication.

Sam Wolfe is a Marketing Futurist, brand strategist, and co-founder and CEO of PitchFWD Reality, a VR/AR consulting firm, and co-founder with Cathy Hackl of The Marketing Futurists, an organization dedicated to preparing Marketers for the next communication tools and technologies.

In addition to running both organizations, Wolfe is an active member of the New York VR/AR community and of the Marketing and Advertising Committees for the VRARA. She speaks on industry panels and manages VR/AR/MR Marketing and Branding Facebook and LinkedIn groups.

Throughout her career, Wolfe has managed B2C and B2B Marketing and branding strategies and creative campaigns for companies such as Showtime Networks, Food Network, Cooking Channel, TV Guide, Rovi (now TiVo), and RLTV. Her team's work on TV Guide won an Effie Award and on Rovi won a European Transform Award.

Sam has her MBA in Marketing, Finance, and Media & Entertainment from NYU Stern School of Business and her BA in Psychology from Yale University.

## ACKNOWLEDGMENTS

CATHY would like to thank the following people for their support, work or inspiration: Katherine Gutierrez, Alejandro Franceschi, Nicole Henderson, Dulce Baerga, Marlon Fuentes, Paola Ariza, Dan Pacheco, Nonny de la Peña, Gemma Busoni, Vanessa Rad, Rob Crasco, Keith Curtin, Charles Babb, Lisa Buyer, Nick Tang, Nick Haase, Dana Dojnik, Annie Eaton, Gaspar Ferreiro, John Buzzell, Gordon Meyer, Rafa Maya, Frank Shi, Jodi Schiller, Iva Leon, Malia Probst, Jonathan Nafarrete, the CyberCode Twins, Jennifer Lee Fader, Stewart Rogers, Megan Lafollett, Beki Winchel, Daniel Contreras, Ryan Steinolfson, Kim Garst, Brian Fanzo, Pam Moore, Jan Barbosa, Rani Mani and the team at Adobe, Manny Ruiz and the Hispanicize team, Ebony Peay Ramirez and the Oculus Launchpad family, Rosario Ballestero-Casas and the team at VR Americas, Emanuel Lombardo, Kris Kolo, Nathan Pettyjohn and the VRARA, Jose Antonio Colchao, the Latin@s in VR AR community, Rodrigo Vergara, Pablo Jenkins and the TEDx Costa Rica team, Hila Raz Harris and Dan Merritts, David Glass, Ana Ruiz, Michael Stelzner, Phil Mershon and the team at SMMW, the Atlanta VR community, Andres Aristizabal, Eddie Israelsky, Erick Lorenzo, Teresita Chavez Pedrosa, Maria Celeste Arrarás, Marta García, Patricia Ramos, Fernando Anzures & the EXMA team, Colleen Seaver and PRSA, Stephen Michael Brown, Amber Aziza, Nicole Walters, Matt Spaulding, Brittney Haynes, Kajal Sachania, Kate Bryant, Lily Garcia, Mayra Cuevas, Jackie Castillo, Glenda Umaña, Susanne Mathieu, Ricardo Varela, Barbara Smith, Brian Wallace, Kim Rose, Jason Nielsen, Nina Thomas, Ruben Vargas, Rafa Mora, Joel Comm, Tyler Anderson, Bryan Kramer, Cesar Restrepo, Tayde Aburto, Ana Reyes, Lizza Monet Morales, Alice Chase, Celeste Martínez, Chayo Garate, Ron Pruett, Shlomi Ron, Marcelo Moyano, Travis Wright, Daniel Sabio, Mitch Jackson, Kathleen Chung, Charles Joekel, the University of Texas at Austin, Belen Moran, Beth Hardy, HTC Vive, and many more.

With all my heart and soul, I would like to also thank my husband Jason and my children Christine, Collin and Camilla for all their love, patience and support on this crazy journey. Thanks to my parents, Luis and Maribel, and my brother and sister-in-law, JuanCa and Cris, for always supporting me and believing in my projects. To all my tias, tios, primos, primas, amigos y amigas in Costa Rica for believing in me. To Marita and Fred, their parents and the rest of the Hackl family for welcoming me into their family. To Aunt Martha and Uncle Steve for your never-ceasing joy. To the Jansen side of the family, a huge thanks for always being there for me. To all the acquaintances, family and friends who have championed me now and throughout the years and led me to where I am today. Most importantly to God almighty for the blessing of being alive.

Sam would like to thank the wonderful Kathleen Chung, the great Gig Barton, the unstoppable Samantha Schonfeld, the incredible Alex Haque, the prolific Jay Van Buren, the helpful John Morse, and the impressively knowledgeable Mark Sternberg for all of their suggestions and feedback. And, to my lovely husband Mike, my ridiculous and hilarious children Maddy, Owen, and Katherine, my amazing in-laws Ray and Ellen, and the spectacular Sandra, thank you for being patient and supportive as I worked on this book. I couldn't have done it without all of you.

Made in the USA
San Bernardino, CA
15 May 2018